Perfect Table

Perfect Table Settings

Hundreds of easy and elegant ideas for napkin folds and table arrangements

Denise Vivaldo

Robert
ROSE

For complete cataloguing information, see page 348.

Disclaimer
The recipes in this book have been carefully tested by our kitchen and our tasters. To the best of our knowledge, they are safe and nutritious for ordinary use and users. For those people with food or other allergies, or who have special food requirements or health issues, please read the suggested contents of each recipe carefully and determine whether or not they may create a problem for you. All recipes are used at the risk of the consumer.

We cannot be responsible for any hazards, loss or damage that may occur as a result of any recipe use.

For those with special needs, allergies, requirements or health problems, in the event of any doubt, please contact your medical adviser prior to the use of any recipe.

Design and Production: Andrew Smith and Joseph Gisini/PageWave Graphics Inc.
Editor: Sue Sumeraj
Recipe Tester: Food Fanatics
Proofreader: Sheila Wawanash
Indexer: Gillian Watts

All interior photography except pages listed below:
Jon Edwards and Associates / © 2010 Denise Vivaldo
Art direction and styling by Denise Vivaldo and Cindie Flannigan

Cover photographer: Colin Erricson
Styling: Charlene Erricson

Page 12: ©iStockphoto.com/Kieran White; 15: ©iStockphoto.com/Lisa Thornberg; 16: ©iStockphoto.com/ Lisa Thornberg; 19: ©iStockphoto.com/Jill Chen; 228: ©iStockphoto.com/Liza McCorkle; 233: ©iStockphoto.com/Robyn Mackenzie; 235: ©iStockphoto.com/Rakoskerti; 239: ©iStockphoto.com/ Magdalena Kucova; 247: ©iStockphoto.com/Pattie Calfy; 251: ©iStockphoto.com/Joe Biafore; 252: ©iStockphoto.com/Matej Pribelsky; 256: ©iStockphoto.com/Lisa Thornberg; 259: ©iStockphoto.com/ Dejan Ristovski; 260: ©iStockphoto.com/Lisa Thornberg; 265: ©iStockphoto.com/Jill Chen; 266: ©iStockphoto.com/RonTech2000; 271: ©iStockphoto.com/Paul Gregg; 272: ©iStockphoto.com/Lisa Thornberg; 334: ©iStockphoto.com/Valentyn Volkov.
Page 320, 331, 346: ©Denise Vivaldo, by Victor Boghossian

We acknowledge the financial support of the Government of Canada through the Book Publishing Industry Development Program (BPIDP) for our publishing activities.

Published by Robert Rose Inc.
120 Eglinton Avenue East, Suite 800, Toronto, Ontario, Canada M4P 1E2
Tel: (416) 322-6552 Fax: (416) 322-6936
www.robertrose.ca

Printed and bound in Canada

1 2 3 4 5 6 7 8 9 TCP 18 17 16 15 14 13 12 11 10

Contents

Acknowledgments

I grew up with a mother who loved to set the table. China, flowers, linens — it didn't have to be a special occasion; at our house, a beautifully set table was an everyday occurrence. Thanks, Mom, for teaching me to enjoy pretty things and sharing your gift of making guests happy and comfortable. This book is as much yours as it is mine.

Writing and completing any book is a team effort. I am grateful that I get to work with so many talented people; otherwise, I wouldn't do it! For me, the two best days of any book deal are the day I sign the contract and the day I hold my first copy of the finished book in my hot, greedy little hands. The days in between are a blur of frustration, elation and exhaustion. I equate writing books to babysitting: I like it best when the baby is clean, quiet and put to bed.

This book could not have happened without my friend Jon Edwards, a talented and generous photographer. Not only did Jon shoot most of the images in this book, but he worked hand in hand with the publisher, sending roughly 2,000 images over the course of six months. He never said, "No, I can't help you today, Denise," even on days when he saw us darkening his studio door with tubs and boxes of napkins and props. Jon's associate at his studio, Heather Winters, a great photographer in her own right, helped us in too many ways to count. I thank you both so very much.

Speaking of us, the nimble and talented hands you see in the how-to napkin fold photos belong to Cindie Flannigan and Jennifer Park, the world's best hand models (and worst-paid) ever! Miss Cindie's nickname is "Busy Hands," and there isn't a napkin she can't wrangle. Many of the napkin folds were Cindie's invention or redesign. Sit her down in front of a stack of napkins and she can't help herself. My napkin fold experience came from my years in catering, where any napkin fold you can teach a waiter in two minutes is a keeper. Our darling assistant, Jennifer Park, tackled many of the more difficult folds. She's still young and limber! You two exceptional women know this book wouldn't have gotten into print without you!

To everyone connected with Robert Rose Publishing, I hope you enjoyed this experience as much as we did. Thank you.

To Lisa Ekus, you and your group rock! I'd be hard-pressed to find a better friend and agent. And thank you, Lisa, for tolerating my complaints all those times I forgot how lucky I am. I should have designed the "Gag fold" for myself.

Thanks to Martha Hopkins for her constant support and unbelievable help. She serves excellent advice with humor, even when the ship is going down. I'm only sorry the captain of the *Titanic* didn't have Martha at his side instead of a band.

To Laura Meyn, Kristen Green Wiewora and Mandy Unruh, please don't change your phone numbers. Martha, Cindie and I need you three!

And last but not least, to my husband, Ken Meyer, a man who appreciates a cloth napkin even when I haven't cooked dinner. As he says, a cloth napkin always gives him hope.

— Denise Vivaldo

Introduction

I grew up setting my family's table. As the youngest of three girls, it was the job that suited me best. Now, even with thousands of parties and photo shoots in my professional past, I still love to set the table! I love dishes, glasses, flowers, place cards and folding napkins. Every part of setting the table is a chance to make the meal more fun, more memorable and more enjoyable. Put a clever party favor at each guest's seat, and you can bet on exclamations of delight.

My life's work as a caterer and food stylist has been all about attention to the details. Setting a pretty table for friends, for family or even just for yourself is an easy way to brighten up your everyday life. I hope this book will inspire you to create a touch of something special for your next party.

Part 1 is all about decorative folds for cloth napkins. In Napkin Folds 101, you'll learn what to look for when you're shopping for napkins, including what fabrics and sizes work best, where to place those perfectly folded napkins and even how to get away with washing your cloth napkins less often (use personalized napkin rings). In 100 Napkin Folds, you'll find step-by-step photographs and detailed instructions for each of — you guessed it — 100 fantastic new and classic napkin folds that will add beauty and whimsy to your table. There's something for everyone, with easy, intermediate and advanced options.

But beautifully folded napkins are just one part of a fabulous table setting. In Table Settings 101, you'll find information on tablecloths, china and glassware, silverware, centerpieces, place cards and party favors. You'll learn how to care for your linens (both tablecloths and napkins), set the table for a sit-down meal and set up a buffet. I've even shared helpful hints on invitations, RSVPs, host or hostess gifts and party etiquette. Then, in 25 Fabulous Table Settings, I show you how to incorporate napkin folds into your overall tabletop decor, with inspirational ideas and photographs for 25 theme parties. These table settings are designed to complement the theme menus in my book *The Entertaining Encyclopedia*, but will also inspire your own menu planning.

When your family and friends arrive for a party and are greeted by a gorgeous table, it's immediately apparent that you've made an effort to put everyone in the mood for a night of fun and celebration. Setting a pretty table might not solve all the ills in the world, but you have to start somewhere. It might as well be your own home!

1
Napkin Folds

Napkin Folds 101

Why take the time for napkin folds? A table set with carefully folded cloth napkins simply makes your guests feel special. Napkin folds certainly add style to the table, but they also warmly evoke the personal touches of another time — one when attention to every detail prevailed over convenience. As a longtime professional caterer and food stylist, it's my job to pay attention to the little details that make a big difference. But there's no reason why you can't do it at home, too. While the popularity of napkin folding comes and goes, I refuse to see it as a lost art. Spend an hour or two with this book, and you can easily teach yourself a number of folds that will help you create a table that is timelessly elegant, retro-funky or up-to-the-minute chic. And if you think napkin folds are only for cruise ships, consider this: adding artfully folded cloth napkins to your tabletop will delight your guests, cost you nothing extra and eliminate disposable paper napkins from your repertoire, greening your entertaining style. How's that for modern?

Choosing the Right Napkins

To get started, all you need is a set of cloth napkins, which you might already have. Otherwise, begin with an easy-on-the-budget set. Medium-weight cotton napkins in a light, neutral color are versatile and chic. If that seems too plain, remember that a fresh flower, place card or wrapped candy tucked into the fold can add color or style to the table when your linens are subtler, as can a napkin ring, colorful ribbon or tassel.

Fabrics

Cloth napkins add sumptuous texture to the table and are more elegant and more absorbent than their paper counterparts. Since you can reuse them for years or even decades, they're environmentally friendly, too. But not all cloth is created equal: napkins come in a number of different fabrics, from 100% linen, cotton or polyester to a variety of blends that attempt to capture the most desirable aspects of each material. Before buying cloth napkins, consider how a particular fabric feels on your hands and face, how well it will go with your china and what kind of care it requires.

Fabric also comes in a variety of weights, from very light to very heavy, and certain weights perform better for certain napkin folds. While a very simple fold can look fuller when done with a thick napkin, a more complicated fold might work better with a thinner napkin that won't get too bulky with multiple folded layers. Each of the 100 napkin folds in this book indicates the weight of fabric it will work best with, so if you have a particular fold in mind, shop for the napkin that will show it off best.

Linen

While a set of white linen napkins, preferably monogrammed, used to be de rigueur for elegant entertaining, linen napkins are usually the most expensive and always require thorough ironing. Linen is made from the flax plant, which has stronger fibers than cotton. Linen is a refined, elegant and cool material, and it's durable; over time and with repeated washings, it will get softer. While linen is infamous for its propensity to wrinkle, it irons to a crisp, cool texture that cotton or polyester can only dream of. If you're lucky enough to have a set of linen napkins, whether new or inherited, use them to add elegance to a special gathering.

Cotton

Absorbent, economical and soft, 100% cotton is probably the most popular choice for cloth napkins for at-home entertaining. While they usually need to be ironed for company, if they're removed from the dryer and folded promptly, many cotton napkins will be presentable for daily family use without ironing. Cotton napkins are also widely available — you'll find them at discount stores as well as high-end retailers, in a variety of colors and patterns, from very elegant to very casual, and in a variety of weights, from light to heavy. Keep in mind that cotton cloth in darker colors will fade with repeated washings, so start with a light neutral.

Polyester

Less absorbent and less sumptuous than their natural-fiber counterparts, polyester napkins can evoke an institutional food-service feel, rougher to the touch than cotton or linen. That said, they can usually be used without ironing, they're resistant to fading and staining, and they're inexpensive. Some polyester fabrics are too soft to hold a crease, though, and are therefore not a good choice for many napkin folds, especially those that are designed to stand upright.

Everyday Cloth Napkins

Some families use cloth napkins every day, taking their commitment to going green so seriously that they even pack cloth napkins in their kids' lunch boxes. For such uses, any cotton napkin will do — lunch boxes are a great venue for mismatched napkins from your own collection or those on sale at home goods stores. It's a good idea to use napkins that aren't special, as one might go missing on occasion.

Blends

As you shop for napkins, you'll find linen-cotton blends and cotton-polyester blends, all of which aim to capitalize on the attributes of each component fabric, whether for color-fastness, texture, thrift or easy care. To keep blends looking their best, always read the care instructions for washing and ironing.

Other Fabrics

Napkins can be made of nearly any fabric. Hemp is gaining momentum; like linen, it's a strong natural fiber, and it's machine-washable. You'll also find silk napkins, which are suitable for some napkin folds, bringing a special sheen to the table.

Colors, Styles and Embellishments

While a crisp white linen or cotton napkin is a great basic supply and works best for the most formal folds, patterns and colors feel less stuffy for many occasions, bringing visual interest to the table and making for stylish folds that fit modern sensibilities. Most of us seek out matching sets of napkins, but a variety of similar patterns can be even more interesting, as can two or more alternating solid colors for larger gatherings. Some hosts even lay out two different folds at each place, making the table setting more dynamic.

When shopping for napkins, in addition to looking at fabric, color and pattern, you'll want to look at the construction of the napkins to determine their quality and suitability for your table. Following are some additional aspects of napkin design to look for.

Make Your Own Embellished Napkins

Bored with a set of neutral cloth napkins? A sewing machine makes quick work of adding trim to napkins, and grosgrain ribbon, colorful rickrack or sassy pom-pom trim will completely change their look. Be sure to prewash both trim and napkins before beginning, as materials can shrink at different rates. While more time-consuming, embroidery is also a great way to embellish cloth napkins.

To add character to napkins without breaking out needle and thread, try fabric markers, which work well on cotton or polyester. These permanent markers can be used freehand or with stencils to add a motif to the edges of napkins or all over them, instantly perking them up. Not much of an artist? Use words to add interest: quotable phrases, poetry, astrological signs and fortune cookie–style admonitions can be written around the edges in any color you choose. Experiment on paper first to make sure you get the spacing as you want it.

Hemmed Edges

Most cotton and linen napkins have hemmed edges, where the edges are folded over and seamed for an elegant finish. Some polyester napkins simply have serged edges, where the edges of the material are bound in thread to keep them from fraying. Hemmed edges look more upscale than serged edges.

Embellished Edges

Some of the most charming vintage linens are embellished with hand-crocheted or lacy edges. Even handkerchiefs with hand-crocheted trim can be folded into quarters to use as cocktail napkins. You'll find many modern versions of napkins with embellished edges too, including those with fringe or beaded trim. Some napkin folds (such as Simplicity, page 98) show off embellished edges better than others, so choose folds that make the most of your napkins.

Hemstitched Napkins

Usually made of linen or hemp, hemstitched napkins are characterized by a wide hem that is attached to the main portion of the napkin with a series of delicate geometric stitches. Hemstitched linens are typically sold in solid colors, and they have a classic, elegant look. They are widely available at retailers such as Pottery Barn (www.potterybarn.com) and Williams-Sonoma (www.williams-sonoma.com).

Damask Napkins

While they can be made of linen, cotton, silk, rayon or even polyester, damask napkins are defined by their woven patterns. Look for a satin weave atop a flat background, usually in the same color, where only the sheen of the fabric reveals the tone-on-tone design. Damask napkins have a very formal look. Their patterns are often intricate floral motifs.

Monogrammed Napkins

Monogrammed napkins bring old-world elegance to the table. While a set of white linen napkins with a white monogram used to be a customary, if very generous, wedding gift, such a set is less commonly found in today's households (outside the Deep South in the United States). If you have your grandmother's set, or you happen upon a vintage set, use them whether or not they bear your own initials — vintage linens are usually very soft and always bring added charm to the table, and an unfamiliar monogram can kick off a fun conversation (who *was* DSS?). Some napkin folds show off a monogram better than others; try Two Points (page 118) for a corner monogram.

Size

Perfectly symmetrical square napkins work best for creating napkin folds. Shoppers will likely notice that, while most cloth napkins are square, not all cloth napkins are the same size; in fact, there doesn't seem to be a universal standard. In general, the larger the meal, the larger the napkin should be. For most of the napkin folds in this book, you'll want a napkin that is at least 20 inches (50 cm) square.

Cocktail Napkins

Used flat as a sort of coaster or folded as a napkin, cocktail napkins can range anywhere from 6 to 13 inches (15 to 33 cm) square. The smaller ones aren't much use for folding, though they make an elegant alternative to paper cocktail napkins when set under a drink.

Luncheon Napkins

Larger than cocktail napkins but smaller than dinner napkins, luncheon napkins range from 12 to 20 inches (30 to 50 cm) square, where they get into dinner napkin territory. Luncheon napkins will work well with some folds, but those on the smaller end aren't usually ample enough for complicated folds.

Dinner Napkins

The largest napkins are the most versatile for napkin folding and can certainly be used at a brunch or lunch as easily as they can at dinner. Dinner napkins are typically 20 to 24 inches (50 to 60 cm) square, although vintage linens and custom-made napkins can be even larger.

Paper Napkins

For the most part, cloth napkins are preferable to paper; they're more absorbent, more eco-friendly and more elegant. But there are times when the convenience of paper napkins will make them your first choice. Paper napkins come in an endless supply of solid colors and colorful patterns, as well as in personalized printed versions that are a nice way to commemorate special occasions such as weddings, anniversaries or reunions.

- **Paper cocktail or beverage napkins** are usually around 5 inches (13 cm) square — about 10 inches (25 cm) when unfolded. These are small enough that they're best left in their folded state and used under drinks.
- **Paper luncheon napkins**, which are typically 6 to 6½ inches (15 to 16 cm) square — or up to 13 inches (33 cm) when unfolded — are the right size and shape for use in place of cloth napkins for certain napkin folds. Some companies offer more

generous dinner-size versions of these napkins, up to 8 inches (20 cm) square when folded. Remember that once you have folded a paper napkin, the crease is there to stay, so practice your fold a few times on the same napkin before getting started on the ones you intend to place on the table. Designs that begin by folding the napkin into a smaller square, such as the Shield (page 94) or even the Bird of Paradise (page 206), are good candidates for paper napkins, because their permanent creases won't detract from the finished design.

- **Paper dinner napkins** are often rectangular, roughly $8\frac{1}{2}$ by $4\frac{1}{2}$ inches (21 by 11 cm) folded. Rectangular napkins won't work for most of the napkin folds in this book. Some paper dinner napkins are square when unfolded; read the package carefully to see whether they're square or rectangular when open. Either way, folded paper dinner napkins can be rolled around flatware and tied with ribbon for a quick version of a buffet roll.

- **Paper guest towels** are similar in size to rectangular paper dinner napkins, but they're a thicker weight, suitable for drying hands. In fact, paper can be preferable to cloth in the guest bath: at larger gatherings where a single cloth towel would be used many times, paper is a more sanitary choice. Paper guest towels can look quite elegant stacked in a basket in your guest bathroom; look for those preprinted with a single initial, as a nod to monogrammed linens.

Napkin Rings

Want to save trees by using cloth napkins every day? Want to save water (and time) by not washing them every day? Give yourself a push in the right direction by investing in some napkin rings. The original intent of monogrammed silver napkin rings was to identify the napkin of each household member so his or her napkin could be reused, avoiding the labor-intensive task of daily laundering. If that bit of history seems fitting for your busy modern life, consider a set of personalized napkin rings for your own family.

Where to Place Napkins on the Table

Back when formal entertaining reigned, the only places you would find a perfectly folded cloth napkin on a set table would be to the left of the forks or atop the plate at each place setting. These days, it seems, anything goes. Depending upon the napkin fold you choose, it might be perched inside the wine or water glasses, hanging over the backs of chairs, nestled inside bowls or wrapped around the silverware. As long as each guest can easily reach his or her napkin and easily use it for its original purpose (no double-knotted ribbons, please), then it works.

While monogrammed silver napkin rings are the classic, there's no need to get that fancy if it doesn't suit your lifestyle. Craft stores such as Hobby Lobby (www.hobbylobby.com) and some Michaels locations (www.michaels.com) carry unfinished wooden napkin rings that can be painted and then personalized. Finished wooden napkin rings are also available at many home goods stores and are easy to personalize: stencil on monogram-style initials or use a paint pen to decorate them in any freehand style you like. If you're not particularly crafty, just look for mismatched napkin rings that will be easy to tell apart, and let each family member choose one, keeping a few extras on hand for overnight houseguests.

For dinner parties, it's helpful to have a larger set of matched napkin rings to give certain napkin folds, such as the Parasol (page 74), a uniform look. You can use classic metal rings or decorative rings, or you can fashion your own napkin rings with raffia, yarn or ribbon tied around the finished napkin fold. Good places to find inexpensive napkin rings are Cost Plus World Market (www.worldmarket.com), Pier 1 Imports (www.pier1.com), T.J. Maxx (www.tjmaxx.com), Marshalls (www.marshallsonline.com), Ross (www.rossstores.com), Target (target.com), Kohl's (www.kohls.com), Tuesday Morning (www.tuesdaymorning.com), Home Outfitters (www.homeoutfitters.com) and HomeSense (www.homesense.ca).

100 Napkin Folds

Knowing how to execute a perfect napkin fold is not a skill everyone has, but it's one you can easily and quickly teach yourself — with the help of this book, of course. These days, anything other than the typical rectangular napkin fold is an uncommon touch for at-home entertaining, yet napkin folds can bring a touch of elegance, whimsy or retro style to your table. And napkin folds take your table setting to the next level with no added expense — you'd have napkins on the table anyway; you're just learning dozens of clever new ways to present them.

Cloth napkins can serve a number of purposes on the table beyond the obvious, acting as placemats, vases or favor bags, for example. No matter which fold you choose — and whether it's on the table for a child's birthday party or a sophisticated dinner party for grownups — the result will make your event more memorable. Like a handwritten thank-you note, napkin folds might be less common than they once were, but they're always noticed, always appreciated and always in style.

The 100 folds that follow are divided into easy, intermediate and advanced sections, so you'll know which ones to start with and how to work your way up. Remember that simpler is sometimes better. The most formal folds, in fact, tend to be relatively easy. And when you're using napkins with an elaborate pattern or design, a simple fold may show it off the best.

While crisp, clean lines are important in the execution of a successful napkin fold, do remember that it's a napkin, not a permanent installation. When your guest sits down, the napkin will be whipped out of shape and draped across a lap, so it doesn't have to be architecturally sound, just a fun but fleeting artistic touch.

Easy Napkin Folds

#①Airplane

Choose a fun multicolored cloth napkin, like the vivid rainbow-hued design I used here, for a whimsical setup, such as for a child's airplane-themed birthday party or the Backyard Campout table setting on page 308. This fold can also bring cool angles to the table for a more grownup sit-down dinner; in that case, select a chic solid-colored cloth napkin. The Airplane fold looks best with pressed napkins; for crisper results, use spray starch.

1 Lay the napkin out as a square, with the finished side facing down and the seamed edges facing up.

2 Fold the lower edge to the upper edge, forming a horizontal rectangle.

3 Holding the center of the lower edge in place with your left hand, use your right hand to fold the right half of the lower edge over to the vertical centerline of the rectangle.

4 Repeat on the left side, folding the lower left edge over to the vertical centerline, forming a triangle.

6 Repeat on the left side, folding the center edge from the vertical centerline down to align with the lower left edge, forming another small triangle.

5 Working with the right side of the triangle, and starting at the vertical centerline, fold the center edge back down to align with the lower right edge, forming a small triangle.

7 Grasping the bottom tip of the large triangle with one hand, use the other hand to gently lift the center of the upper edge so that the smaller triangles at the left and right come in to meet at the vertical centerline.

8 Flatten the lifted fabric into a narrow center triangle that overlaps the small triangles at either side, forming a paper airplane shape.

#2 BBQ Bib

Some meals are beyond messy. Use an actual barbecue bib or a checkered kitchen towel instead of a napkin for this fold, which suits Southern-style barbecue or seafood boils especially well. The finished fold will look best with medium- to heavyweight fabric, such as the red and white checked bib I used here. Iron bibs or towels lightly without spray starch before folding.

1 Lay out barbecue bib or kitchen towel vertically, with any ties at the bottom.

2 Fold the left edge over toward the right edge, slightly less than one-third the width of the bib or towel.

3 Fold the right edge over toward the left edge, slightly less than one-third the width of the bib or towel, overlapping the previous fold.

4 Fold the upper edge down to the lower edge, leaving any ties exposed at the bottom.

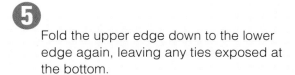

5 Fold the upper edge down to the lower edge again, leaving any ties exposed at the bottom.

6 Arrange the napkin with any ties (or the open end) at the top.

#❸Bikini

This flirty napkin fold looks just like a bikini bottom, so it's the perfect choice for a summer cocktail party or poolside cookout. Choose a fun, vibrant fabric in any weight, like this napkin with multicolored citrus slices. Iron napkins with spray starch before folding; there's no need to press after folding.

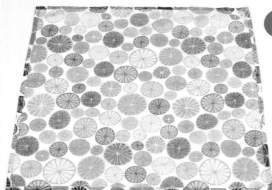

❶ Lay the napkin out as a square, with the finished side facing down and the seamed edges facing up.

❷ Fold the right edge over to the left edge, forming a vertical rectangle.

❸ Fold the lower right and lower left corners in to meet in the center, forming a point at the bottom of the napkin.

❹ Flip the napkin over, keeping the point down.

5 Fold the upper right and upper left corners in to meet in the center, forming a point at the top of the napkin.

6 Fold the upper half of the napkin down over the lower half, leaving about 1 inch (2.5 cm) of the lower half exposed.

7 Fold the upper edge of the napkin down about 2 inches (5 cm), covering where the bottom triangle begins and creating a band on top.

#❹ Bird in Flight

This fold is so named because it looks as if it's about to take off into flight. You can use just about any napkin: any weight, fabric, pattern and color will work. Here, I chose a white napkin with maroon and brown flowers. Iron napkins with spray starch before folding. After folding, gently press the tail for a tailored look or leave it as is for a more casual look.

❶ Lay the napkin out as a square, with the finished side facing down and the seamed edges facing up.

❷ Fold the upper right corner down to the lower left corner, forming a triangle.

❸ Fold the lower right point up to the upper left point, forming a smaller triangle.

❹ Fold the lowest point up to the highest point, forming an even smaller triangle and arranging the triangle with the loose folds at the top.

5 Fold the upper right point toward the left, using slightly more than two-thirds the width of the napkin and aligning the upper edges.

6 Fold the upper left point back over to the right, aligning the folds at the left edge and allowing the tip to hang past the right edge.

7 Tuck the top 2 inches (5 cm) underneath the napkin, leaving the tail pointing out from the upper right side.

8 Arrange the napkin with the tail at the bottom.

#⑤ Bird's Nest

This little nest will delight guests, and it makes the perfect base for presenting small party favors at each place. Another option is to top each nest with a small bird, whether an edible marshmallow chick in the springtime or a decorative bird ornament come winter. Any fabric weight in any color or pattern will work. Here, I used a yellow napkin with a multicolored leaf pattern. Iron napkins without spray starch before folding.

① Lay the napkin out as a square, with the finished side facing down and the seamed edges facing up.

② Fold the lower right corner up to the upper left corner, forming a triangle.

③ Fold the upper left corner down to the middle of the triangle's right side.

④ Fold the upper left edge halfway down to the lower right edge.

⑤ Fold the upper left edge down to the lower right edge, forming a long, narrow napkin.

6 Pick up napkin, with loose edges facing up. Twist the napkin three complete times.

7 Using about half the total length of the twisted napkin, form it into a circle, overlapping the ends.

8 Wrap the loose ends of the napkin around the circle, tucking the tips into the folds of the twisted napkin, forming a nest.

9 Arrange a nest flat at each place.

#6 Bouquet

This fold is tied with a ribbon, adding girlish style to the tabletop. Alternatively, you can pull it through a napkin ring. If using ribbon, keep in mind that you will need a 20-inch (50 cm) length for each napkin. Any fabric weight in any color or pattern works; I used a crisp white napkin with a bright multicolored daisy pattern on it and tied it with green- and white-checked ribbon, which would be perfect for a springtime brunch. Press napkins before folding.

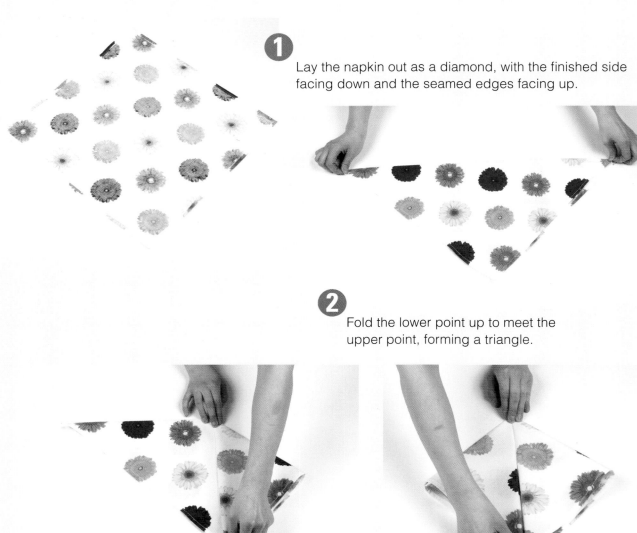

1 Lay the napkin out as a diamond, with the finished side facing down and the seamed edges facing up.

2 Fold the lower point up to meet the upper point, forming a triangle.

3 Fold the left point up to the upper point.

4 Fold the right point up to the upper point, forming a diamond.

5 Wrap a ribbon around the napkin, placing it about one-quarter of the way up from the bottom of the napkin and tying it firmly in a single knot.

6 Tie the ribbon into a bow. Fan out the top layers of fabric.

7 Arrange the napkin with the ribbon at the top or the bottom.

#**7** Bow

This pretty bow is a great fold for ladies' brunches or lunches, baby showers, bridal showers or anytime you want to bring fun feminine style to the table. I used a solid-colored napkin in a muted yellow hue and paired it with a metal napkin ring. Look for fabrics that contrast with your china, in any color or pattern, and a coordinated napkin ring or tie to hold the bow in place. Stick with light- to medium-weight fabrics so the fold won't be too thick to fit in a napkin ring. Press napkins lightly before folding, but skip the starch in favor of a more flowing look.

1 Lay the napkin out as a diamond, with the finished side facing down and the seamed edges facing up.

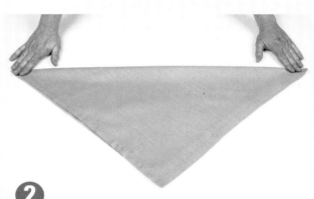

2 Fold lower point of patterned diamond up to upper point of patterned diamond, forming a patterned triangle atop a solid diamond.

3 Fold the lower point up to the upper point, forming a triangle.

4 Fold the lower edge of the napkin up enough to just cover the lower tip of the small triangle.

5 Fold the upper edge of the napkin down to the lower edge.

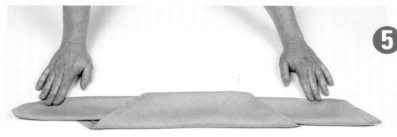

6 Repeat on the other side, using your left hand to fold the left point of the napkin over at an upward angle, making the fold about 2 inches (5 cm) shy of the napkin's vertical centerline and pointing the tail toward the upper right.

7 Holding the center of the lower edge with your left hand, use your right hand to fold the right point of the napkin over at an upward angle, making the fold about 2 inches (5 cm) shy of the napkin's vertical centerline and pointing the tail toward the upper left.

8 Pinch the center of the fold together with one hand while holding a napkin ring in the other.

9 Slide the napkin ring over the fold, positioning it in the center.

10 Arrange the bow and tails as necessary. Flip the bow over and arrange it on a plate.

#**8** Bowtie

Simple but very polished-looking, this fold is great for use with napkin rings or ribbons. It works with any color or pattern in almost any fabric weight. I chose brown napkins with purple stripes. Avoid using napkins that are too thick, as the multiple folds will make them difficult to fit through a napkin ring. Iron napkins with spray starch before folding. If the meal requires a pair of chopsticks, slide them between the finished fold and the napkin ring.

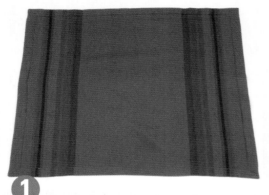

1 Lay the napkin out as a square, with the finished side facing down and the seamed edges facing up.

2 Fold the lower edge up to the horizontal centerline of the napkin.

3 Fold the upper edge down to the horizontal centerline.

4 Fold the right edge just past the vertical centerline of the napkin.

5 Fold the left edge just past the vertical centerline.

6 Fold the lower edge up about 2 inches (5 cm).

7 Fold the upper edge down about 2 inches (5 cm).

8 Flip the napkin over, keeping the rectangle horizontal. Pinch the middle of the upper edge and lower edge together to form a bow.

9 Slide napkin ring to middle of bow to secure it.

10 If using chopsticks, slide them between the napkin ring and the bow. Present a bow vertically at each place, adjusting the ends as necessary.

#❾Buffet Roll

This roll is a neat way to bundle utensils and napkins together, making it easy for your guests to pick up everything they'll need at the end of a buffet line. This fold works with any fabric weight in any color or pattern, but keep in mind that both sides of the fabric will show in the finished roll, so choose something that's attractive on both sides, such as the beige napkin I used here. Iron napkins with spray starch before folding, and tie the finished fold with ribbon to keep utensils securely in place. You'll need a 20-inch (50 cm) length of ribbon for each napkin.

① Lay the napkin out as a square, with the finished side facing down and the seamed edges facing up.

② Fold the lower right corner up about halfway to the center of the napkin.

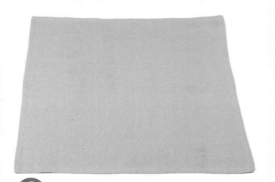

③ Fold the upper edge of the napkin down to the lower edge, forming a horizontal rectangle.

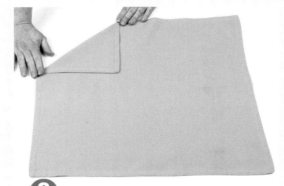

④ Fold the left edge over to the right edge, forming a square.

⑤ Fold the upper left and right corners in toward the center.

6 Fold the lower left corner in toward the center.

7 Fold the upper right edge down toward the lower left edge just far enough to cover the point.

8 Fold the lower left edge up to the upper right edge.

9 Flip the napkin over, arranging the point at the top.

10 Slide flatware into the pocket and tie the napkin with a ribbon to secure it.

#⑩Burro

You'll need two napkins in slightly different sizes for this attention-grabbing fold — and two napkins per person can be very handy for messy meals. (Fajitas, anyone?) Use light- to medium-weight fabrics in contrasting, festive colors. I paired an orange napkin with a larger, fringed green napkin and placed the finished fold in a beer glass, leaving the ends of the napkin to stick up, looking like two tall burro ears. You can also tie the bottom of the fold with twine or ribbon and lay it flat on each plate. This fold works best with unstarched napkins.

❶ Lay the smaller napkin out as a square, with the finished side facing down and the seamed edges facing up. Top with the larger napkin, centering it over the first, with the finished side facing down and the seamed edges facing up.

❷ Rotate the napkins so that they're laid out as a diamond. Fold the lowest corner up to the center of the napkin.

❸ Working from the flat fold at the lower end of the diamond, roll napkins up together until you reach the end.

4 Have a beer glass ready as you pick up the napkin from the middle.

5 Fold the napkin in half and drop the folded end into the glass.

6 Arrange the napkin fold so that the ears point up evenly.

#⑪Clutch

In the shape of a chic clutch purse, this napkin fold works well with medium- to heavyweight fabric in a feminine pattern, such as the napkin with green and ivory flowers and vines I used here. Decorate the finished fold with a pearl, button or other decorative object to mimic a purse closure. For a completely different look, use a napkin in a bold solid color and call the fold an envelope; use a sticker or foil seal for the closure (see the black envelope on page 305). Either way, iron the napkins with spray starch before folding; after folding, leave as is for a casual look or press gently for crisp lines.

① Lay the napkin out as a square, with the finished side facing down and the seamed edges facing up.

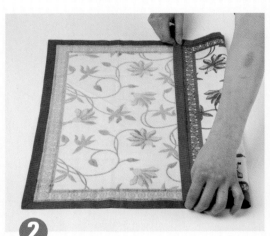

② Fold the left edge in to the vertical centerline of the napkin.

③ Fold the right edge in to the vertical centerline.

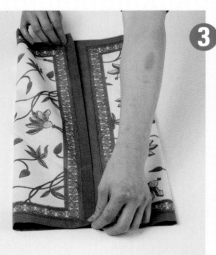

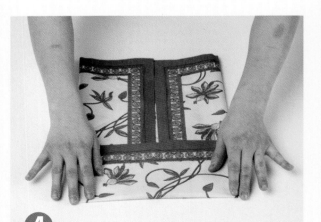

④ Fold the upper edge down to the horizontal centerline of the napkin.

5 Fold the lower edge up to the horizontal centerline.

6 Fold the lower left and right corners in to meet in at the center of the bottom half, forming a point.

7 Fold the point up over the top half of the napkin, forming a clutch shape.

8 Arrange the napkin with the point down. Place a pearl, button or other decorative object where the clutch closure would be.

#12 Crown

This regal fold is fit for celebrating the king or queen of the day, so choose a color worthy of royals, such as the solid red used here — or perhaps lavender or pink for a princess. This fold works best with medium- to heavyweight fabrics ironed with spray starch before folding, because the fabric needs body to stand up (though the crowns can also be displayed flat). Just for fun, place a small treat under the napkin fold to surprise guests.

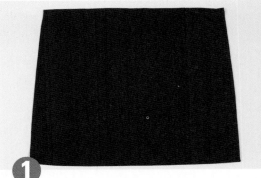

1 Lay the napkin out as a square, with the finished side facing down and the seamed edges facing up.

2 Fold the lower edge up to the upper edge, forming a horizontal rectangle.

3 Fold the right edge down to the lower edge.

4 Fold the left edge up to the upper edge.

5 Flip the napkin over and arrange it horizontally.

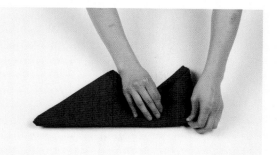

6 Fold the lower edge up to the upper edge, leaving a small triangle dangling on lower left side.

7 Flip the napkin over, arranging it with the triangle still pointing down, but now on the right side. Fold down the small triangle on the left. Fold the left point of the napkin over toward the right, using about one-third the width of the napkin fold and tucking the point under the top layer of fabric.

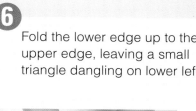

8 Flip the napkin over again, keeping the points down. Fold the left point of the napkin over toward the right, tucking the point under the top layer of fabric.

9 Place flat or stand the crown up, pulling the sides gently apart to create a circular form.

#**13** Cup Kerchief

Perfect with hot soups or stews, as well as oversize lattes, this cup kerchief acts as a cozy for the bowl or mug, giving it more style as well as protecting hands from the heat. I chose a blue and white fruit print here (see pages 306 and 307 for other examples), but any fabric weight in any color or pattern works with this fold, so choose something that suits the occasion. Iron napkins with spray starch before folding.

1 Lay the napkin out as a square, with the finished side facing down and the seamed edges facing up.

2 Fold the upper left corner down to the lower right corner, forming a triangle.

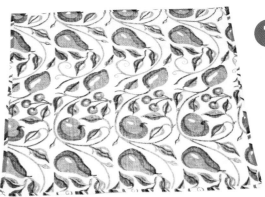

3 Fold the upper left edge down toward the lower right corner, creating a roughly 2-inch (5 cm) wide band.

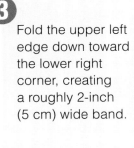

4 Wrap the band around a bowl or coffee mug, lacing it through hte handle, if there is one.

5 Tie the two tails into a firm single knot around the bowl or mug.

6 Arrange the triangular kerchief as desired.

#**14** Diamonds

A two-sided woven fabric, such as this black napkin with light stripes, works best for the Diamonds fold, because both sides of the napkin will be visible in the finished presentation. Any fabric weight works well. Iron with spray starch before folding; after folding, gently press for a tailored look or leave as is for a more casual look.

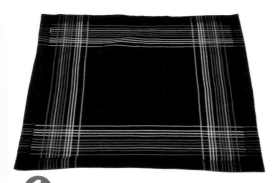

1 Lay the napkin out as a square, with the finished side facing down and the seamed edges facing up.

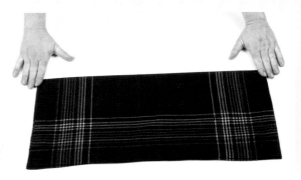

2 Fold the lower edge up to the upper edge, forming a horizontal rectangle.

3 Fold the right edge over to the left edge, forming a square.

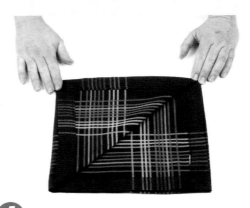

4 Fold the top layer of the upper left corner down to the lower right corner, forming a diagonally divided square.

5 Fold the next layer of the upper left corner down to the center of the napkin, forming a small triangle in the upper left quadrant of the napkin.

6 Fold the top layer of the lower right corner up to the center of the napkin, forming a small triangle in the lower right quadrant of the napkin.

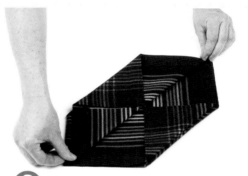

7 Tuck the remaining bottom layers of the lower right corner under the napkin, aligning the edges with the folded top layer.

8 Tuck the remaining bottom layers of the upper left corner under the napkin, aligning the edges with the folded top layer. Arrange the napkin horizontally on a plate.

#15 Divided Fan

The showy look of this fold is completed with a tie or napkin ring, which gives you another opportunity to incorporate the party's theme. I tied mine off with a piece of raffia and a sand dollar, but you can use any decorative ribbon or yarn, perhaps with a favor or bauble attached. Use a medium- to heavyweight fabric in any color or pattern. I chose a brown napkin with a black pattern. Iron napkins with spray starch before folding, and be sure to have your ties or napkin rings ready before you begin. Use 12-inch (30 cm) lengths if you'll be tying a knot or 20-inch (50 cm) lengths if you'll be tying a bow.

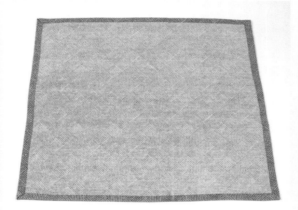

1 Lay the napkin out as a square, with the finished side facing down and the seamed edges facing up.

2 Fold the lower edge up to the horizontal centerline of the napkin.

3 Fold the upper edge down to the horizontal centerline.

4 Fold the left edge over toward the right, forming a vertical band about 1½ inches (4 cm) wide.

5 Fold the band under, aligning the left edges.

6 Fold the band back over, aligning the left edges.

7 Continue folding the band, accordion-style, until you reach the right edge of the napkin.

8 Turn the napkin so that the pleats are facing up and use a tie, ribbon or napkin ring to secure the center.

9 Fan out the folds to create a double fan.

#⓰ Divided Square

This easy napkin fold is suitable for any occasion and any fabric weight. I chose a traditional ivory and dark red toile napkin here, but you can try this fold with solid, patterned or striped napkins. Iron napkins with spray starch before folding. After folding, gently press for a tailored look or leave as is for a more casual look. To personalize each place, tuck a place card into the opening on this fold. For a different presentation, rotate the square so it's a diamond instead.

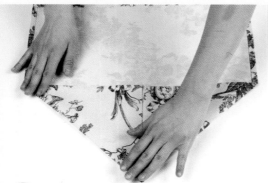

1 Lay the napkin out as a square, with the finished side facing down and the seamed edges facing up.

2 Fold the upper left corner to the center of the napkin.

3 Fold the upper right corner to the center.

4 Repeat with the lower left and lower right corners, forming a diamond.

5 Rotate the napkin so that it's laid out as a square. Grip the napkin at the center of both the left and right sides.

6 Carefully lifting the napkin from the sides, tuck the upper half under the lower half, forming a rectangle.

7 Fold the left half over the right half, forming a divided square.

#17 Double Ring

This rolled design brings its understated curves to any place setting. Depending upon the napkin, it could be very formal or informal — you can even set a patio table with this napkin fold for the Neighborhood Block Party table setting on page 282. Choose a light- to medium-weight fabric in any design. Napkins with a decorative border are shown off to their best advantage in this fold.

1 Lay the napkin out as a square, with the finished side facing down and the seamed edges facing up.

2 Fold the upper edge down to the horizontal centerline of the napkin.

3 Fold the lower edge up to the horizontal centerline, forming a horizontal rectangle.

4 Flip the napkin over, keeping it arranged as a horizontal rectangle.

5 Starting at the right edge, roll up the napkin toward the center.

6 Continue rolling until you reach the vertical centerline of the napkin.

7 Beginning at the left edge, roll up the napkin toward the center.

8 Continue rolling until the left roll meets the right roll in the center.

#18 Duet

This two-napkin fold is easier than it looks. Use silky napkins for a formal look or cotton napkins for a casual table. Medium- to heavyweight fabrics ironed with spray starch work best. Place the napkin fold in a stemmed glass for visual appeal.

1 Use two complementary napkins.

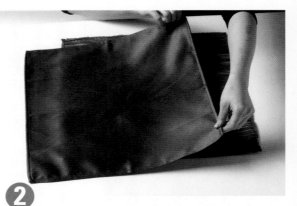

2 Lay the napkins out as a square, with the finished sides facing down and the seamed edges facing up.

3 Line up the napkins so that the edges are aligned.

4 Gather both napkins at the center by placing one hand underneath and pressing the napkins down into your palm with the other hand.

5 Gather about 4 inches (10 cm) together into a loose point.

6 Place the gathered point inside a wineglass or other glass. Pull apart the ends and arrange them as desired.

#**19** Fan

Use a small bowl or mug, or even a takeout box (as on the bottom of page 61), to anchor this easy fold. I chose a solid black napkin and a turquoise blue bowl, but you can use any fabric weight in any color or pattern for this design. Iron napkins with spray starch before folding. Have one container per napkin ready before you begin folding.

1 Lay the napkin out as a square, with the finished side facing down and the seamed edges facing up.

2 Fold the lower edge up to the upper edge, forming a horizontal rectangle.

3 Fold the left and right edges over about 1½ inches (4 cm).

4 Fold the left and right edges under about 1½ inches (4 cm), aligning the folds at each side.

5 Fold the left and right edges back over about 1½ inches (4 cm), aligning the folds at each side.

6 Fold the left and right edges back under about 1½ inches (4 cm) so that they meet under the center of the napkin.

7 Fold the left and right sides together to finish the accordion-style fold.

8 Place the narrow end of the napkin (the one that shows more layers of fabric) in a container, bending it around the bottom of the container to anchor it.

9 Spread out the top of the napkin fold to create a fan effect. Arrange a fan at each place.

#20 Fir Tree

Create this easy, fun fold for Christmas, Earth Day or any other party theme that might call for a tree-shaped napkin. To help it stand upright, look for medium- to heavyweight fabrics, and starch and press them before folding. For tree-like results, I chose a solid green napkin, but any solid or pattern will work. For a holiday table, add a Christmas ornament as a favor on each tree — or place a star on top.

1 Lay the napkin out as a square, with the finished side facing down and the seamed edges facing up.

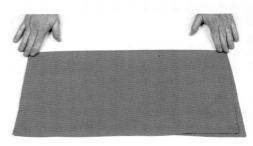

2 Fold the lower edge up to the upper edge, forming a horizontal rectangle.

3 Fold the upper left and lower left corners in to the horizontal centerline, forming a point on the left side.

4 Fold the upper right and lower right corners in to the horizontal centerline, forming a point on the right side.

5 Fold the left point in to the center of the napkin.

6 Fold the right point in to the center, forming a square.

7 Gripping all layers in the center, gently pick up the napkin.

8 Tuck the upper and lower edges in toward the center, forming an upright napkin fold with four points.

9 Arrange the four points.

#**21** Fortune Cookie

The Fortune Cookie fold can be placed flat on a plate or displayed upright, with a handwritten fortune tucked inside for each guest. While it would be great for a home-cooked Asian meal, this fold can also elevate takeout. The design works well with fabrics of any weight, color and pattern; I chose a solid aqua napkin. Iron napkins with spray starch before folding; after folding, gently press for a tailored look or leave as is for a more casual look.

1 Lay the napkin out as a diamond, with the finished side facing down and the seamed edges facing up.

Fold the upper point down to the lower point, forming a triangle.

3 Holding the middle of the upper edge with your right hand, use your left hand to fold the left point down to the lower point.

4 Fold the right point down to the lower point, forming a diamond.

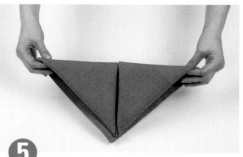

5 Carefully picking up the napkin from the right and left corners, fold the lower half of the diamond under the upper half, forming a triangle.

6 Gently bring the lower right and left points closer together, raising the napkin to an upright position.

7 Position the napkin on an angle at each place, adding a fortune, if desired.

#22 Gypsy Skirt

This fold looks like a festive multilayered skirt. Use napkins with decorative borders or trim to take full advantage of this cute design; I chose an orange napkin with pink rickrack. Any fabric weight will work well; iron with spray starch before folding. After folding, gently press for a tailored look or leave as is for a more casual look.

1 Lay the napkin out as a square, with the finished side facing down and the seamed edges facing up.

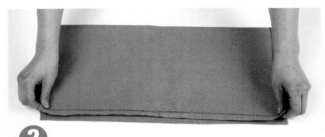

2 Fold the lower edge up to the upper edge, forming a rectangle.

3 Fold the left edge over to the right edge, forming a square.

4 Rotate the napkin so that it's laid out as a diamond, with the loose points at the bottom. Fold the top two layers of the lower point up to the upper point, so that the trim shows around the entire diamond.

5 Fold the top layer of the upper point down toward the lower point, just far enough to leave about 1 inch (2.5 cm) of the bottom of the diamond exposed.

6 Fold the next layer of the upper point down toward the lower point, just far enough to leave about 1 inch (2.5 cm) of the previous layer exposed.

7 Fold the last layer of the upper point down toward the lower point, just far enough to leave about 1 inch (2.5 cm) of the previous layer exposed.

8 Flip the napkin over, keeping the large point down. Fold the left and right sides in at a slight downward angle, overlapping them.

9 Flip the napkin over again and arrange it with the points down.

#23 Hobo Sack

When you want to bundle up a little party favor for your guests, this fold is a great way to do it (see page 250 for some favor suggestions). The loose, easygoing form of this fold means it will work with any color or pattern in any fabric weight; I chose a red and white checked napkin. I used a wooden clothespin to hold it closed, but you could tie the top with ribbon instead. Iron napkins with spray starch before folding. Have one clothespin, or a 20-inch (50 cm) length of ribbon, and one favor ready for each.

1 Lay the napkin out as a square, with the finished side facing down and the seamed edges facing up.

2 Fold in the lower left and lower right corners, using a little more than one-third the width of the napkin on each side.

3 Fold in the upper left and upper right corners, using a little more than one-third the width of the napkin on each side. Place a favor in the center of the napkin.

4 Gather together the upper and lower flat edges.

5 Holding the upper and lower edges together, add the right flat edge to the gathered edges.

6 Holding the upper, lower and right edges together, add the left flat edge to the gathered edges.

7 Secure all four sides at the top with a clothespin or a ribbon. Arrange the corners of the sack as necessary for the best presentation.

#24 Liner

You could use this fold for napkins at each place, of course, but its flat form also makes it great for stacking between plates at a buffet table or for lining bread baskets. The Liner fold works with any color or pattern in any fabric weight; here, I chose a solid dark gold napkin. Iron napkins with spray starch before folding. After folding, gently press for a tailored look or leave as is for a more casual look.

1 Lay the napkin out as a square, with the finished side facing down and the seamed edges facing up.

2 Fold the upper edge down to the lower edge, forming a horizontal rectangle.

3 Fold the right edge over to the left edge, forming a square.

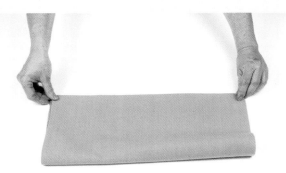

4 Fold the top layer of the left edge back toward the right edge, using one-third the width of the napkin.

5 Fold the newly created middle fold over just beyond the right edge, forming a vertical rectangle atop the napkin.

6 Fold the left edge halfway to the vertical rectangle.

7 Fold the left edge over just beyond the right edge.

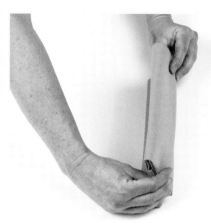

8 Flip the napkin over, keeping the same loose edges down.

9 If necessary, adjust the napkin so that all three layers show.

#25 Loot Bag

Who doesn't like loot? I sure do! This easy napkin fold can hold a party favor or it can be the party favor: fill it with candy that suits your party theme, or even chocolate coins. It works with any color or pattern in any fabric weight; here, I used a red bandana tied with twine (see opposite for a black skull-and-crossbones version). Iron napkins with spray starch before folding. Prepare a 12-inch (30 cm) length of twine or ribbon for each napkin tie or, if you will be tying a bow, prepare a 20-inch (50 cm) length.

1 Lay the napkin out as a square, with the finished side facing down and the seamed edges facing up.

2 Lift the lower right and lower left corners and pinch them together above the napkin.

3 Add the upper left and upper right corners, holding them together above the napkin, forming a bag with four soft points.

4 Holding the points together, tie twine or ribbon a few inches below the tips, securing the bag.

5 Arrange the corners of the loot bag as necessary for the best presentation.

#26 Parasol

This perky parasol is so showy, yet so easy to fold. I chose a fresh-looking green striped napkin tied with a green organza ribbon, but you could use any striped or patterned medium-weight fabric and any coordinating ribbon. As an alternative to ribbon, try jute or yarn for a rustic look, or simply pull the end through a napkin ring. For crisp results, iron napkins with plenty of spray starch before you get started. Prepare a 20-inch (50 cm) length of ribbon for each napkin.

1 Lay the napkin out as a square, with the finished side facing down and the seamed edges facing up.

2 Fold the lower edge of the napkin up about 1½ inches (4 cm).

3 Fold the lower edge under about 1½ inches (4 cm), aligning the lower edges.

4 Continue folding the lower edge over and under in 1½-inch (4 cm) bands, accordion-style, until you reach the top of the napkin.

5 Place one hand in the center of the napkin and use the other hand to fold it in half lengthwise.

6 Wrap a ribbon around the napkin about 2 inches (5 cm) from the folded side.

7 Turn the napkin so that the pleats are facing up and tie the ribbon into a tight bow.

8 Fan out the top of the napkin.

#27 Placemat

This tidy fold makes a small square placemat suitable for use under a salad, luncheon or dessert plate. With oversized napkins, you can create a placemat large enough for a dinner plate. The underside of the napkin will show in the finished fold, so choose a fabric that's pretty on both sides, like the pastel striped napkin here. Any fabric weight works with this fold. Iron napkins with spray starch before folding. After folding, gently press for a tailored look or leave as is for a more casual look.

1 Lay the napkin out as a square, with the finished side facing down and the seamed edges facing up.

2 Fold the lower left corner up to the center of the napkin.

3 Fold the lower right corner up to the center.

4 Fold the upper left corner down to the center.

5 Fold the upper right corner down to the center.

6 Flip the fold over, arranging it as a square. Fold the lower right corner up to the center.

7 Fold the lower left corner up to the center.

8 Fold the upper left corner down to the center.

9 Fold the upper right corner down to the center.

10 Flip the napkin over, arranging it as a square. Working in the upper left quadrant, fold the point from the center of the square back to the upper left corner, forming a triangle.

11 Repeat in the remaining three quadrants, folding each point from the center of the square back to the outside corner.

#28 Pleat

This casual napkin fold results in a tall design with a pleat running down the middle. It works well with any fabric weight. Use a solid or striped napkin, such as the bright red one I used here. Napkins with stripes can have a different look depending on whether you start with the stripes running vertically or horizontally. The fold would also be fun with napkins that have a contrasting reverse side, since the pleat will show a narrow band of the napkin's underside. Iron the napkins with spray starch before folding. After folding, gently press them for a tailored look or leave as is for a more casual look.

1 Lay the napkin out as a square, with the finished side facing down and the seamed edges facing up.

2 Fold the lower edge up about 3½ inches (8.5 cm), forming a horizontal band at the bottom of the napkin.

3 Continue folding the napkin up the same amount and in the same direction, folding about three more times, until you get to the upper edge of the napkin.

4 Flip the napkin over. Lift the top layer of the upper edge and fold the seamed portion back about ½ to ¾ inch (1 to 2 cm). Fold it in the same direction one more time, creating a narrow band that shows the reverse side of the fabric.

6 Arrange the napkin as a vertical rectangle.

5

Pick the napkin up from the center and fold it in half lengthwise.

#29 Pocket

A pocket filled with flatware is the perfect presentation for picnics and casual parties. After placing utensils in each pocket, you can even tie it with twine or ribbon and stack the filled napkins in a basket for picking up at the end of a buffet line. To play up the casual country feel of this fold, I used a blue and white checked napkin, but any fabric weight in any color or pattern will work. Iron napkins with spray starch before folding. After folding, gently press for a tailored look or leave as is for a more casual look.

1 Lay the napkin out as a square, with the finished side facing down and the seamed edges facing up.

2 Fold the lower edge up about 3 inches (7.5 cm), forming a horizontal band at the bottom of the napkin.

3 Fold the upper edge down to meet the edge of the previous fold.

4 Flip the napkin over, keeping the same sides up and down. Fold the right edge in to the vertical centerline of the napkin.

5 Fold the left edge in to the vertical centerline.

6 Fold the left edge over to the right edge.

7 Arrange the napkin with the larger rectangle at the bottom.

8 Slide the silverware for each place setting into the pocket.

#③⓪ Pope's Hat

This elegantly easy fold can grace the most formal tables. It looks great in classic white or any other solid-color medium- to heavyweight fabric. Here, I chose a rust red napkin with faint brocade stripes. The simplicity of the Pope's Hat makes it a great choice for embellishment with a decorative item, such as the gold star shown at the bottom of page 83. Iron napkins with spray starch before folding. After folding, gently press for a tailored look

① Lay the napkin out as a diamond, with the finished side facing down and the seamed edges facing up.

② Fold the upper point down to the lower point, forming a triangle.

③ Fold the left point down to the lower point, aligning the edges at the lower left side.

④ Fold the right point down to the lower point, forming a diamond.

5 Fold the top quarter of the diamond under, creating a flat edge at the top of the napkin.

6 Fold the left point underneath the napkin to meet the vertical centerline, forming a vertical edge on the left side.

7 Fold the right point underneath the napkin to meet the vertical centerline, forming a vertical edge on the right side. Gently pull apart the two lower points to expose the middle point. Arrange the napkin on a plate with the points facing up.

#31 Pull-Through

This simple fold is designed for a napkin ring. Its looseness lends it to casual entertaining, as does the blue and white checked napkin I used here. Any napkin ring will work; choose something that complements your napkins and theme. This design works with any color or pattern in any fabric weight. Iron napkins with spray starch before folding.

1 Lay the napkin out as a square, with the finished side facing down and the seamed edges facing up.

2 Fold the lower right corner up toward the upper left corner, positioning it slightly above and to the right of the upper left corner, forming two offset triangles.

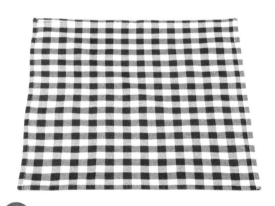

3 Fold the upper right corner down toward the lower left corner, positioning it slightly above and to the left of the lower left corner.

4 Holding the point at the center of the right side of the napkin, fold the upper half of the napkin down over the lower half, aligning the layers at the lower right edge.

5 Pull the right point of the napkin through a napkin ring, positioning the ring halfway up the napkin.

6 Arrange the napkin with the tip pointing down.

#32 Ring Roll

This quick and easy roll is perfect for use with napkin rings, and it works with any fabric weight, color and pattern. Here, I used a silky brown napkin paired with a brass rope napkin ring. You'll find other examples of the Ring Roll on pages 262, 282 and 336. Iron napkins before folding — there's no need to use spray starch.

1 Lay the napkin out as a square, with the finished side facing down and the seamed edges facing up.

2 Fold the right edge over to the left edge, forming a vertical rectangle.

3 Fold the lower edge up to the upper edge, forming a square.

4 Beginning at the upper edge, loosely roll the napkin down to the lower edge.

6 Arrange the napkin roll seam side down, adjusting the ring as necessary.

5 With the folded edges at the top of the roll and the loose edges at the bottom, slide a napkin ring onto the roll, positioning the ring at the middle of the roll.

#33 Rocket

Talk about dramatic: you'll create instant height on your table with this upright fold. It works with any solid-color or patterned fabric, such as the yellow-green napkin with bright stripes I chose. To help it stand up, choose a medium- to heavyweight fabric and iron napkins with spray starch before folding to give them extra body.

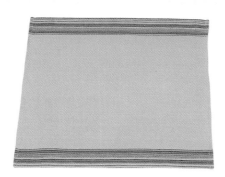

1 Lay the napkin out as a square, with the finished side facing down and the seamed edges facing up.

2 Fold the upper right corner down to the lower left corner, forming a triangle.

3 Fold the upper right edge down about 1 inch (2.5 cm), creating a band on the longest side of the triangle.

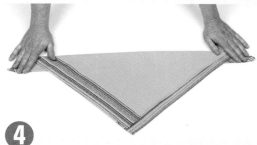

4 Flip the napkin over, positioning the longest side of the triangle at the bottom.

5 Fold the top point down to the middle of the lower edge.

6 Leaving a 1-inch (2.5 cm) band at the top of the napkin, fold the middle point back up.

8 Beginning at the left edge, roll the napkin up all the way to the right point.

7 Fold the left point over toward the right point, using one-third the width of the lower edge and aligning the lower edges.

9 Tuck the right point into the band at the base of the napkin to secure it.

10 Stand the rocket up on its base. Fold the outer layer of the top tip down, forming a downward-pointing triangle.

11 Arrange a rocket upright at each place.

#34 Rosebud

For picnics or buffets, I like placing a basket of these napkins next to the plates. Any fabric weight in any color or pattern works. To play up the rosebud look, choose a solid-color napkin that complements the occasion (red for Valentine's Day, white for a bridal shower, yellow for a birthday party). Or choose a fun floral print, as I did here with a multicolored daisy pattern. Iron napkins with spray starch before folding.

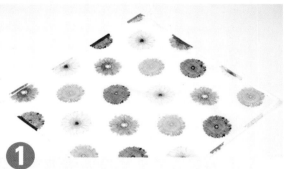

1 Lay the napkin out as a diamond, with the finished side facing down and the seamed edges facing up.

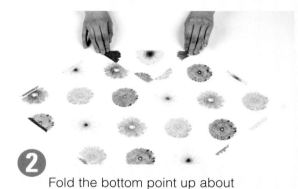

2 Fold the bottom point up about 4 inches (10 cm).

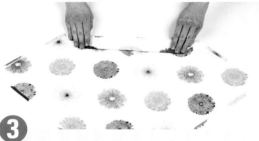

3 Fold the lower edge up almost to the point.

4 Continue folding up six or seven more times, until you reach the top of the napkin.

5 Turn the napkin to a vertical position. Starting at the end closest to you, begin rolling it up.

6 Continue rolling until you reach the top.

7 Tuck the loose point securely into the nearest fold.

8 Stand the rosebud upright on its base and carefully pull layers of napkin up from the center, creating a petal-like effect.

Nancy

#35 Sailboat

This fun, casual design is suitable for either kids or adults. I chose a blue, green and white wavy-striped napkin to play up the nautical theme. The fold will work with solids, patterns or stripes in all fabric weights. Iron napkins with spray starch before folding. After folding, gently press for a tailored look or leave as is for a more casual look.

1 Lay the napkin out as a square, with the finished side facing down and the seamed edges facing up.

2 Fold the upper right point down to the lower left point, forming a triangle.

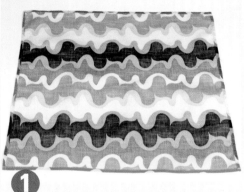

3 Rotate the triangle so that the longest side is at the top, with the middle point down.

4 Holding the bottom point with your right hand, use your left hand to fold the left point up until the edges run up the vertical centerline of the napkin.

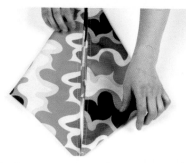

5 Holding the bottom point with your left hand, use your right hand to fold the right point up until the edges run up the vertical centerline of the napkin.

6 Fold the upper left tip of the napkin down so that the fold is flush with the fold beneath it and the right edges align in the center of the napkin.

7 Fold the upper right tip of the napkin down so that the fold is flush with the fold beneath it and the left edges align in the center of the napkin.

8 Using the top third of the napkin, fold the upper edge down at a slight angle, giving the boat a jaunty look.

#36 Shield

This easy fold can go formal with an elegant solid-colored napkin or fun with a whimsical patterned fabric, such as the white, green and yellow lemon napkin I used. It works best with medium- to heavyweight fabric. Iron with spray starch before folding. After folding, gently press for a tailored look or leave as is for a casual look. Tuck a place card or a small favor into the pointed pocket, if you like.

1 Lay the napkin out as a square, with the finished side facing down and the seamed edges facing up

2 Fold the lower edge up to the upper edge, forming a horizontal rectangle.

3 Fold the left edge over to the right edge, forming a square.

4 Fold the lower left corner just past the center of the napkin.

5 Flip the napkin over, positioning it with the new flat side at the bottom. Fold the left and right sides in, overlapping them to create a shield shape with a flat bottom.

6 Flip the napkin back over and arrange it with the points up.

#37 Simple Upright

It doesn't get any easier than this. Dress up a plain napkin with a decal or sticker, then use a simple fold to show it off. (Arts and crafts stores, such as Michaels, offer a variety of decals and stencils that can add style to your table linens.) You can also leave the embellishment off and simply lean a place card against the napkin fold. The Simple Upright fold works with any color or pattern in any fabric weight. Here, I used a pale yellow napkin with a gold bird decal. Iron napkins with spray starch before folding. Lightly press after folding, taking care to avoid ironing any decorations.

1 Lay the napkin out as a square, with the finished side facing up and the seamed edges facing down. Add a decal near the lower edge of the napkin, just to the left of the vertical centerline.

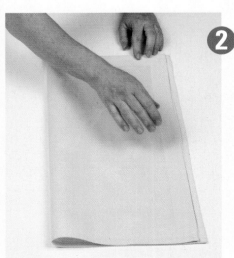

2 Flip the napkin over so that the finished side is facing down, keeping the decal at the lower edge. Fold the left edge over to the right edge, forming a vertical rectangle.

3 Fold the left edge over to the right edge again, forming a narrower rectangle with the decal showing just above the lower edge.

4 Fold the upper edge underneath the napkin to meet the lower edge.

5 Again fold the upper edge underneath the napkin to meet the lower edge, forming a small square. Separate the top and bottom layers to stand the napkin upright.

#38 Simplicity

Show off napkins with lace edges to their best advantage with this elegant fold, in which two decorative edges grace the entire front length. It's a lovely design for any casual or formal occasion. Any fabric weight works. I chose an ivory napkin with an embroidered border. Iron napkins with spray starch before folding. After folding, gently press for a tailored look or leave as is for a more casual look.

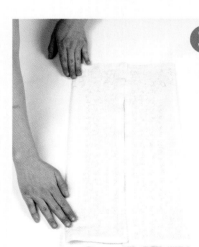

1 Lay the napkin out as a square, with the finished side facing down and the seamed edges facing up.

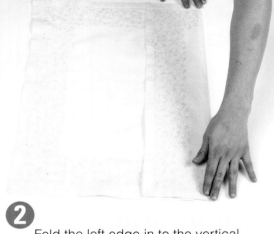

2 Fold the left edge in to the vertical centerline of the napkin.

3 Fold the right edge in to the vertical centerline.

4 Flip the napkin over, leaving it as a vertical rectangle. Fold the left edge in to the vertical centerline.

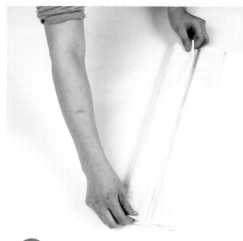

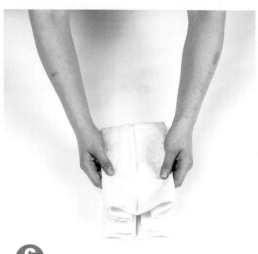

5 Fold the right edge in to the vertical centerline.

6 Fold the lower edge up to the upper edge. Arrange the napkin with the loose edges at the bottom.

#39 Simply Skinny

Present this simple fold plainly, as shown here, pull it through a napkin ring or dress it up with a decorative clip. Here, I chose a solid yellow napkin, but the fold will be pretty with any color or pattern in any fabric weight. Iron napkins with spray starch before folding. After folding, gently press for a tailored look or leave as is for a more casual look.

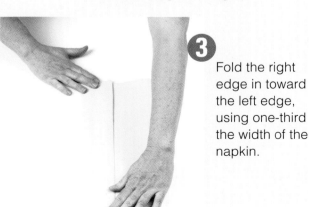

1 Lay the napkin out as a square, with the finished side facing down and the seamed edges facing up.

2 Fold the left edge over to the right edge, forming a vertical rectangle.

3 Fold the right edge in toward the left edge, using one-third the width of the napkin.

4 Fold the left edge over to the right edge, forming a skinny vertical rectangle.

5 Fold the lower edge up to the upper edge.

6 Arrange the napkin with the loose edges at the bottom.

#⓴ Single Wing

Simple and elegant, this design works for any sit-down meal, from fancy to casual. Choose a muted solid napkin for more elegant meals or any color or pattern for more festive ones. I used a tan napkin with a wide white border, which is shown off nicely in the finished fold. Medium- to heavyweight fabric works best for this fold, which needs the bulk to stand up successfully. To stiffen the fabric further, starch and iron napkins well before folding.

1 Lay the napkin out as a square, with the finished side facing up and the seamed edges facing down.

2 Fold the lower edge up to the upper edge, forming a horizontal rectangle.

3 Fold the right edge over to the left edge, forming a square.

4 Fold the upper left corner down to the lower right corner, forming a triangle.

5 Working with the top two layers of fabric, fold the lower right corner back toward the upper left corner, forming a small square atop the napkin fold.

6 Slide the upper right and lower left points toward each other, lifting the middle of the napkin to stand it upright.

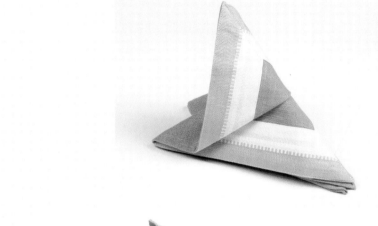

7 Arrange the napkin on an angle at each place.

#41 The Standard

This is the napkin fold of the typical family dinner. Make it special by using starched and ironed cloth napkins, such as the beige hemstitched napkin shown here. Any color or pattern and any fabric weight will work. After folding, gently press for a tailored look or leave as is for a more casual look. Place the finished napkin atop each plate, if you like.

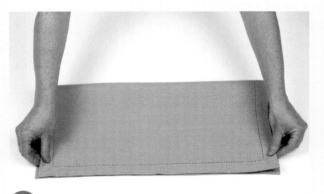

1 Lay the napkin out as a square, with the finished side facing down and the seamed edges facing up.

2 Fold the lower edge up to the upper edge, forming a horizontal rectangle.

3 Fold the right edge over to the left edge, forming a square.

4 Flip the napkin over, keeping the same edges at the top and bottom. Fold the right edge over to the left edge.

5 Arrange the napkin with the loose edges at the right and lower edges.

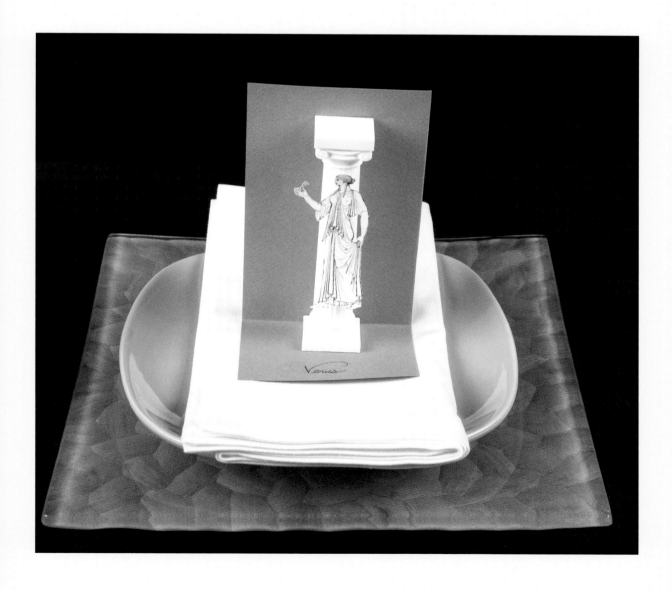

#42 Three Flags

Easy and elegant, this fold can be used with any fabric weight in any color or pattern. I chose a solid medium blue napkin. Iron napkins with spray starch before folding, and press again after folding. This fold can be draped over the back of each chair or over the edge of the table at each place setting.

1 Lay the napkin out as a square, with the finished side facing down and the seamed edges facing up.

2 Fold the lower right corner up to the upper left corner, forming a triangle.

3 Fold the lower left point up just above and to the left of the upper right point, forming two smaller offset triangles.

4 Fold the left point over toward the right points, placing it just above and to the left of them, forming three smaller offset triangles.

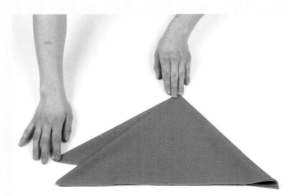

5 Tuck the left side of the top triangle under the napkin to form a narrower stack of triangles.

6 Arrange the napkin fold with the three points down.

#43 Three-Fold

This fold really shows off napkins with wide decorative borders, such as this gorgeous Provence-inspired yellow napkin with red flowers. The finished napkin fold has three triangles, hence the name. Any fabric weight will work, although thicker napkins will need to be pressed after folding to lie flat. Iron napkins with spray starch before folding.

1 Lay the napkin out as a square, with the finished side facing down and the seamed edges facing up.

2 Fold the right edge over to the left edge, forming a vertical rectangle.

3 Fold the lower edge up to the upper edge, forming a square.

4 Fold the upper left point down to the lower right point, forming a triangle.

5 Flip the napkin over and fold the center point over to touch the middle of the opposite side. Press as necessary and arrange vertically.

#44 Tie One On

This simple napkin fold isn't necessarily one you'll use at each place setting, but it's perfect for dressing up any serving piece with a handle, from wicker baskets to trays to beer steins. It works well with any color or pattern in any fabric weight, and will even work with slightly smaller luncheon napkins. I used a white napkin with a bright daisy pattern. Iron napkins with spray starch before folding.

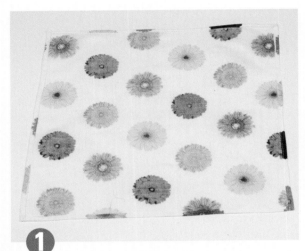

1 Lay the napkin out as a square, with the finished side facing down and the seamed edges facing up.

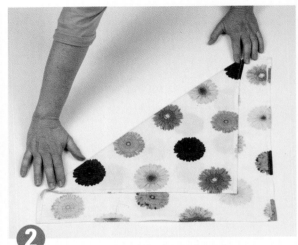

2 Fold the lower right corner up toward the upper left corner, leaving 2 to 3 inches (5 to 7.5 cm) of the bottom layer exposed.

3 Fold the upper left point down to the middle of the lower right edge.

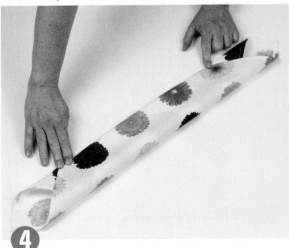

4 Fold the upper left edge down to the lower right edge.

5 Gripping the upper left and lower right sides together to make a narrow strip, pick up the napkin.

6 Lace one end of the napkin through the handle of a serving piece.

7 Tie the napkin into a single knot.

8 Arrange the serving piece to show off the tied handle.

#45 Tray Roll

This roll makes a neat way to bundle utensils and napkins together, which is especially handy if you're placing them on a tray for a meal away from the table. These rolls are also great placed at the end of a buffet line; in that case, use lengths of raffia or ribbon to hold them together. Here, I chose a red and green striped tea towel that would be perfect for Christmas, but this rolled-up design works well with any color or pattern in any fabric weight. Iron tea towels or napkins with spray starch before folding.

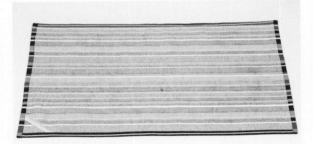

1 Lay the napkin out flat, with the finished side facing down and the seamed edges facing up.

2 Fold the lower edge up toward the upper edge, using one-third the height of the napkin.

3 Fold the upper edge down to the lower edge, forming a narrow horizontal rectangle.

4 Place utensils on top of the napkin, about one-quarter of the way in from the right edge. Align the handles of the utensils just above the lower edge of the napkin.

5 Fold the right edge over the utensils.

6 Starting from the right edge, roll up utensils until you reach the end of the napkin.

7 Arrange utensils at each place. For buffets, tie rolls closed with raffia or ribbon.

#46 Trifold

I used a silky brown napkin for this simple fold, which shows off, in its three layers, the lustrous sheen of the fabric. This fold can be left as is or gathered with the use of a napkin ring, as in the photo on the bottom of page 115. Use any fabric weight in any color or pattern. This fold looks best if the napkins are ironed with spray starch before folding; after folding, gently press for a tailored look or leave as is for a more casual look.

1 Lay the napkin out as a square, with the finished side facing down and the seamed edges facing up.

2 Fold the lower edge up toward the upper edge, using one-third the height of the napkin.

3 Fold the upper edge down to the lower edge, forming a horizontal rectangle.

4 Fold the left edge about 2 inches (5 cm) to the right, forming a vertical band.

5 Pick up the vertical band and fold another vertical band under it and offset to the right of the original band.

6 Pick up both vertical bands and fold a third vertical band under them and offset to the right of the second band.

7 Fold the right edge over to meet the closest vertical band.

8 Flip the napkin over.

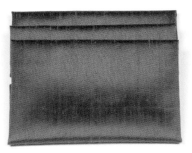

9 Arrange the napkin with the bands at the top.

#47 Tulip

Like a few other designs in this book, the Tulip fold can be arranged flat at each place or stand upright, bringing height to your place settings. To help it stand up, choose a medium- to heavyweight fabric and lightly starch it before ironing. I chose a multicolored tropical flower print, which suits the Hawaiian Luau table setting on page 318. Try it with a solid-color napkin for a formal dinner or, for a more casual table, with any pattern that coordinates with your theme.

1 Lay the napkin out as a diamond, with the finished side facing down and the seamed edges facing up.

2 Fold the upper point down to the lower point, forming a triangle.

3 Fold the right point down to the lower point.

4 Fold the left point down to the lower point, forming a diamond.

5 Flip the napkin over, keeping the same point up.

6 Fold the upper point down toward the lower point, leaving about 2 inches (5 cm) of the bottom layer showing.

7 Flip the napkin over again, keeping the same point down. Fold the left side over toward the right side, using about one-third the width of the napkin.

8 Fold the right side over to the left edge, overlapping the previous fold.

9 Tuck the tip of the fold under the top layer of the previous fold to secure it.

10 Flip the napkin over and arrange it with the point up.

11 Alternatively, open up the base and arrange the napkin standing upright.

#48 Two Points

This easy fold can take on a very formal appearance when done with a white napkin, or can be more festive when a color or pattern is used. I like using napkins with a decorative border, such as this beige napkin with white edging, to play up the fold's two points. Any fabric weight will work. Iron napkins with spray starch before folding. After folding, gently press for a tailored look or leave as is for a more casual look.

1 Lay the napkin out as a diamond, with the finished side facing down and the seamed edges facing up.

2 Fold the lower point up toward the upper point, leaving about 2 inches (5 cm) of the bottom layer showing.

3 Flip the napkin over, keeping the same point up. Holding the middle of the lower edge with your right hand, use your left hand to fold the left point up toward the upper point, so that the inner edge of the fold creates a vertical centerline.

4 Fold the right point up toward the upper point until the inner edge of the fold meets the vertical centerline.

5 Flip the napkin over, keeping the same points up and down. Fold the lower point up about 2 inches (5 cm).

6 Flip the napkin over again, keeping the same flat edge down. Fold the lower left diagonal edge over to meet the vertical centerline.

7 Fold the lower right diagonal edge over to meet the vertical centerline.

8 Flip the napkin over and arrange it with the flat edge up.

#49 Two Tails

This elegant, easy presentation will work with any fabric weight, in any color or pattern; white is the most formal-looking. Here, I used a warm orange linen hemstitched napkin. Dress it up with a tassel or other decorative object, if you like (as in the photo on the bottom of page 121). Iron napkins with spray starch before folding. After folding, gently press for a more tailored look or leave as is for more casual results.

1 Lay the napkin out as a square, with the finished side facing down and the seamed edges facing up.

2 Fold the upper left point down to the lower right point, forming a triangle.

3 Fold the left point over to the lower right point, aligning the lower edges.

4 Fold the upper right point down to the lower right point, forming a square.

5 Fold the upper left corner under the napkin toward the lower right corner, using one-third the length of the diagonal of the square.

6 Fold the left edge over to meet the diagonal centerline (or past it for smaller plates).

7 Fold the upper edge over to meet the diagonal centerline (or past it for smaller plates).

8 Flip the napkin over. Arrange it on the plate with the tips pointing up or down.

#50 Vase

This fold makes a cute container for a silk flower at each place setting (you could use a fresh flower, but keep in mind that it won't be in water and add it at the last minute so it doesn't wilt). Slightly smaller napkins work better than larger ones. Any fabric weight will do. Choose a color and pattern that suits the occasion; fringed or lacy edges will be shown off to their best advantage in this design. I used a lavender and white checked napkin with a fringed edge. Iron napkins with spray starch before folding. After folding, gently press for a tailored look or leave as is for a more casual look.

1 Lay the napkin out as a diamond, with the finished side facing down and the seamed edges facing up.

2 Fold the lower corner up to the upper corner, forming a triangle.

3 Fold the left point up to the upper point.

4 Fold the right point up to the upper point, forming a diamond.

5 Fold the lower left edge over to the vertical centerline.

6 Fold the lower right edge over to the vertical centerline, forming a kite shape.

7 Working with the top layer only, fold the upper left point down.

8 Working with the top layer only, fold the upper right point down.

9 Flip the napkin over. Fold the top point down, aligning the top edge with the folded layers beneath.

Intermediate Napkin Folds

#51 Basket

Perfect for any spring or summertime brunch or lunch, especially one held outside on the patio, the Basket fold can be presented on its own or with a place card, flower or sprig of herbs tucked into one of its many folds. Choose a cloth napkin in any pattern or color that coordinates with your party theme. I chose a bright yellow patterned napkin with a solid border, which shows up nicely in the finished fold. Be sure to use napkins that are pretty on both sides, as both sides will be visible in the finished design.

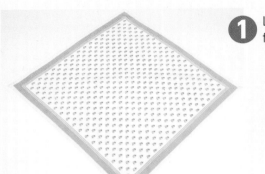

1 Lay the napkin out as a diamond, with the finished side facing up and the seamed edges facing down.

2 Fold the lower left edge up to the upper right edge, forming a rectangle.

3 Fold the lower right edge up to the upper left edge, forming a diamond.

4 Tuck the top layer of the upper point under to meet the inside of the lower point.

5 The napkin will now have a visible horizontal centerline.

6 Tuck the next layer of the upper point under just far enough to leave a 1-inch (2.5 cm) band above the horizontal centerline.

7 Fold the next layer of the upper point over so that the finished side of the fabric shows, tucking the point under the previous layer just far enough to leave a 1-inch (2.5 cm) band above the previous band.

8 Flip the napkin over, keeping the same point up. Holding the lower point with your left hand, use your right hand to fold the lower right edge in at an angle, about two-thirds of the way to the vertical centerline.

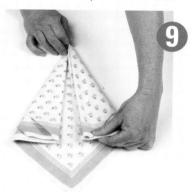

9 Holding the lower point with your right hand, use your left hand to fold the lower left edge in at an angle, about two-thirds of the way to the vertical centerline.

10 Fold the lower tip up, using about one-third the height of the napkin.

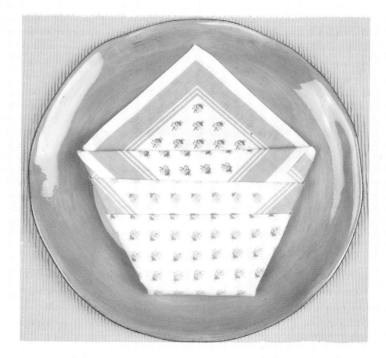

11 Flip the napkin over and arrange pointed side up at each place.

#52 Bunny

What could be more fitting for Easter dinner or a springtime brunch than this cute fellow placed atop each plate? Add candy or button eyes to the finished Bunny fold to make it even more recognizable. Any color or pattern will do; for springtime parties, think white or solid pastels, such as the pale yellow napkin I used here. It's best to use a lightweight fabric so that the ears stay folded. Iron napkins with spray starch before folding, and press gently after folding.

1 Lay the napkin out as a square, with the finished side facing down and the seamed edges facing up.

2 Fold the lower edge up to the horizontal centerline of the napkin.

3 Fold the upper edge down to the horizontal centerline.

4 Fold the lower edge up to the upper edge, forming a thin horizontal rectangle.

5 Holding the middle of the lower edge in place with your left hand, use your right hand to fold the lower edge of the right half up to the vertical centerline of the napkin.

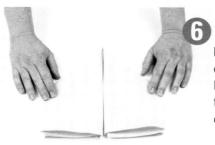

6 Fold the lower edge of the left half up to the vertical centerline.

7 Fold the upper right corner down, forming a triangle on the right side.

8 Fold the upper left corner down, forming a diamond.

9 Fold the upper right edge of the diamond in to meet the vertical centerline.

10 Fold the upper left edge of the diamond in to meet the vertical centerline.

11 Flip the napkin over. Arrange at each place with ears up.

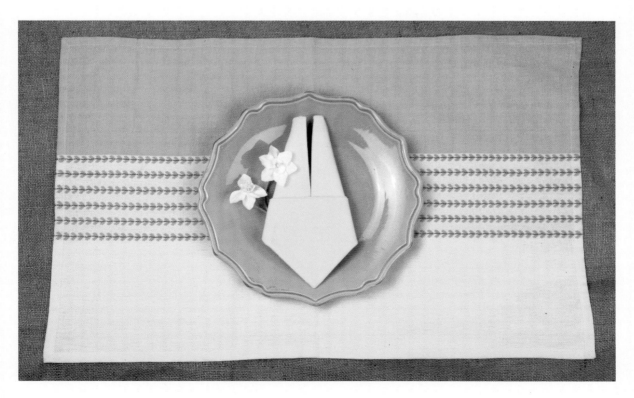

#53 Cabbage Rose

This gorgeous fold is easier than it looks; once you get the hang of it, you'll be able to create these quickly. Because this design has a pretty, feminine, floral look, try it for the Girls' Night In table setting on page 300 or for any occasion that's girls-only or has a female guest of honor. Use a medium-weight fabric, lightly starched and ironed, in any color or pattern. The Cabbage Rose design gives you a great way to present a flower blossom, a small favor or even a roll, muffin or scone at each place.

1 Lay the napkin out as a square, with the finished side facing down and the seamed edges facing up.

2 Fold the lower left and right corners in to the center of the napkin.

3 Fold the upper left and right corners in to the center of the napkin, forming a diamond.

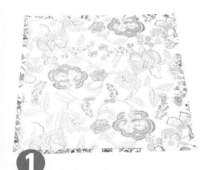

4 Fold the right point in to the center of the napkin.

5 Fold the left point in to the center of the napkin.

6 Fold the upper and lower points in to the center of the napkin, forming a square.

7 Fold the lower left and right corners in to the center of the napkin.

8 Fold the upper left and right corners in to the center of the napkin, forming a diamond.

9 Flip the diamond over and arrange it as a square. Fold the upper right corner in to the center of the napkin.

10 Fold the remaining three corners in to the center of the napkin, forming a diamond.

11 Holding the center of the diamond steady with your left hand, use your right hand to reach underneath the upper point and find the center point beneath it. Gently pull that point out to form a petal.

12 Repeat on the remaining three points. Holding the center of the diamond steady with one hand, use the other hand to reach underneath each point and find the center point beneath it. Gently pull each center point out to form a petal.

13 Holding the center of the napkin steady with your right hand, use your left hand to reach underneath the upper left edge and find the center point beneath it. Gently pull that point out and up, forming a petal.

14 Repeat on the remaining three edges. Holding the center of the napkin steady with one hand, use the other hand to reach underneath each edge and find the center point beneath it. Gently pull each center point out and up to form a petal. Arrange a cabbage rose at each place.

#54 Clown Hat

You don't have to be a kid to get a kick out of this cute fold. While it can be left flat on the plate, it's a lot more fun when presented standing up, so choose a medium- to heavyweight fabric that will stay upright. It also helps to iron the napkins with spray starch before folding them. This design is most festive with a fun patterned fabric, like the green napkin with big brown polka dots I used here. Surprise your guests by hiding a little something underneath each napkin.

1 Lay the napkin out as a square, with the finished side facing down and the seamed edges facing up.

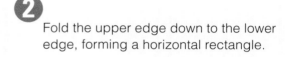

2 Fold the upper edge down to the lower edge, forming a horizontal rectangle.

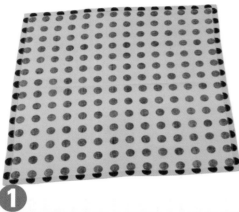

3 Holding the middle of the upper edge with your right hand, use your left hand to fold the upper left corner down, creating a slim triangle with a roughly 3-inch (7.5 cm) base atop the napkin. Smooth the fold.

4 Continuing to hold the middle of the upper edge with your right hand, pick up the newly folded upper left edge and fold it over again, making the fold the same width as the previous one.

5 Fold the triangle over again so that the right edge meets the vertical centerline.

6 Fold two more times, heading toward the other end of the napkin.

7 Fold the triangle one last time to reach the end of the napkin, aligning the end of the napkin with the edge of the triangle.

8 Rotate the napkin so that the point is facing you.

9 Reach into the base of the triangle and turn the bottom third inside out, forming a cone.

10 Open the cone up so that it stands upright. Stand a clown hat upright at each place and arrange the points as necessary.

#55 Cowl

The Cowl fold is simple and elegant, and it has a little opening that could hold a small favor or a piece of candy. Try it with a solid blue, white or aqua napkin (as I used here) for the Grecian Get-Together table setting on page 336. For any other sit-down dinner party, select a fabric in a color or pattern that complements your theme and setting. This fold works best with large lightweight napkins; starch and press them before you begin.

1 Lay the napkin out as a square, with the finished side facing down and the seamed edges facing up.

2 Fold the upper edge down toward the lower edge, using one-third the height of the napkin.

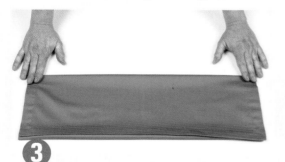

3 Fold the lower edge up to the upper edge, forming a horizontal rectangle.

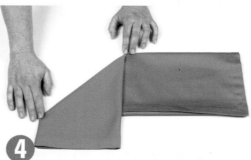

4 Holding the middle of the lower edge with your left hand, use your right hand to fold the right half of the lower edge up almost to the vertical centerline of the napkin.

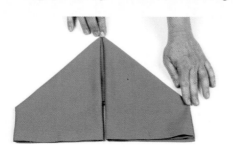

5 Fold the left half of the lower edge up almost to the vertical centerline, leaving a small gap in the middle.

6 Flip the napkin over, keeping the point down and the tails up.

7 Fold the upper edge of the right tail down to almost meet the top of the triangle.

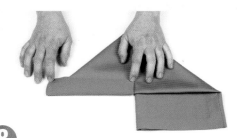

8 Fold the right tail down again, forming a band on top of the right side of the triangle.

9 Fold the upper edge of the left tail down to almost meet the top of the triangle. Fold the left tail down again, forming a band on top of the left side of the triangle.

10 Placing one hand atop each band, pull the bands down to meet under the triangle.

11 Arrange the bands parallel to each other, flat on the work surface, with the triangle extending up.

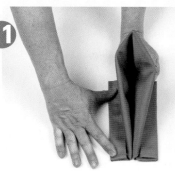

12 Curl the triangle around to one side to form a round opening. Arrange at each place with the opening facing down.

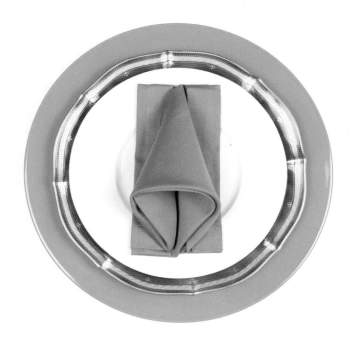

#56 Diagonal

Use double-sided napkins to enjoy the full impact of this fold, which shows off both sides in alternating diagonal bands. I used a brown floral napkin with a coordinating stripe on the reverse side. Any fabric weight will work. Iron napkins with spray starch before folding. After folding, gently press for a tailored look or leave as is for a more casual look.

1 Lay the napkin out as a square, with the finished side facing down and the seamed edges facing up.

2 Fold the lower edge up to the upper edge, forming a horizontal rectangle.

3 Fold the top layer of the upper edge back down, leaving a 2-inch (5 cm) band of fabric showing below the edge.

4 Fold the remaining layer of the top edge down over the newly folded edge, creating an upper band that's the same width as the lower one, about 2 inches (5 cm) tall.

5 Flip the napkin over so that the previous fold is at the lower edge. Fold the lower left corner up to the horizontal centerline, forming a small triangle on top of the napkin.

6 Using the right edge of the triangle as a guide, fold the left side over toward the right side.

7 Fold the upper right corner down to the horizontal centerline, forming a small triangle on top of the napkin.

8 Using the left edge of the triangle as a guide, fold the right side over toward the left side.

9 Fold the lower right corner up to the center of the upper edge, forming a triangle on top of the napkin.

10 Fold the upper left corner down to the center of the lower edge, forming a parallelogram.

11 Flip the napkin over and arrange it horizontally.

#57 Double Envelope

This fun fold makes a lovely base for name tags or party favors. It works best with medium- to heavyweight fabrics, such as this pretty multicolored blue, white and green floral napkin. A portion of the napkin's underside will show in the finished fold, so choose a fabric that's pretty on both sides. Iron with spray starch before folding. After folding, gently press for crisp results. The finished fold works well arranged vertically, horizontally or even diagonally on each plate.

1 Lay the napkin out as a square, with the finished side facing down and the seamed edges facing up.

2 Fold the lower edge up to the upper edge, forming a horizontal rectangle.

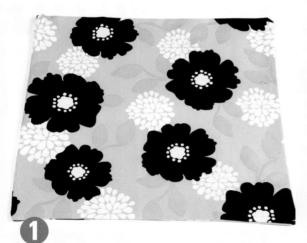

3 Fold the left edge over to the right edge, forming a square.

4 Fold the top layer of the upper right corner down to the lower left corner, creating a triangle on top of the square.

5 Fold the top layer of the lower left corner into the center of the napkin, creating a smaller triangle.

6 Fold the top layer of the upper right corner into the center of the napkin, creating another small triangle.

7 Tuck the upper left corner under to the center of the napkin.

8 Tuck the lower right corner under to the center of the napkin.

#58 Double Pleats

This sweet and versatile fold works well with fabric in any weight, color and pattern, resulting in a small diamond shape with two pleats running up the middle. I chose a rusty orange napkin with a small calico print, for a country look. Iron napkins with spray starch before folding. After folding, gently press for a tailored look or leave as is for a more casual look.

1 Lay the napkin out as a square, with the finished side facing down and the seamed edges facing up.

2 Fold the upper edge down toward the lower edge, using one-third the height of the napkin.

3 Fold the lower edge up to the upper edge, forming a horizontal rectangle.

4 Holding the middle of the lower edge with your right hand, use your left hand to fold the left half of the lower edge up to the vertical centerline of the napkin.

5 Fold the right half of the lower edge up to the vertical centerline.

6 Flip the napkin over, keeping the point down and the tails up. Fold the upper edge of the left tail down to meet the top of the triangle.

7 Fold the left tail down again, forming a band on top of the left side of the triangle.

8 Fold the upper edge of the right tail down to meet the top of the triangle. Fold the right tail down again, forming a band on top of the right side of the triangle.

9 Flip the napkin over, keeping the point down. Holding the middle of the upper edge with your right hand, use your left hand to fold the left side down so that the band meets the vertical centerline.

10 Fold the right side down so that the band meets the vertical centerline. Arrange the napkin vertically or horizontally on a plate.

#59 Exploding Envelope

This elaborate-looking fold can be arranged flat at each place or stand upright for an even more dramatic presentation. It would be striking for the Wine and Cheese Tasting table setting on page 296, or anytime you want to bring height to your place settings. Choose a medium- to heavyweight fabric and lightly starch and press napkins before you begin folding. Solid colors keep the focus on its striking folded form, so avoid using busy patterns for this design — I chose a bright gold napkin here.

1 Lay the napkin out as a diamond, with the finished side facing down and the seamed edges facing up.

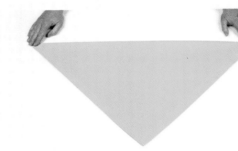

2 Fold the lower point up to the upper point, forming a triangle.

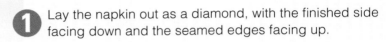

3 Holding the middle of the lower edge with your left hand, use your right hand to fold the right point up to the upper point.

4 Fold the left point up to the upper point, forming a diamond.

5 Fold the lower point up toward the upper point, leaving about 2 inches (5 cm) of the bottom layer showing.

6 Working with the top layer only, fold the center point down to the lower edge of the napkin.

7 Working with the right side of the upper point, fold the top layer down to the lower edge of the napkin, tucking it under the top fold.

8 Working with the left side of the upper point, fold the top layer down to the lower edge of the napkin, tucking it under the top fold.

9 Fold the top layer of the upper point down, tucking it under the previous layer, leaving a small band showing at the top.

10 Flip the napkin over, keeping the same point up. Fold the right point over toward the left, using one-third the width of the napkin and creating a vertical right edge.

11 Fold the left point over toward the right, using one-third the width of the napkin and creating a vertical left edge. Tuck the left point into the pocket at the right to secure it.

12 Flip the napkin over and arrange it with the point up. Alternatively, open up the base and arrange the napkin standing upright.

#60 Fish

This whimsical napkin fold is fun for kids and adults — think pool party, a seafood menu or even Chinese takeout (the fish is a symbol of abundance in Chinese culture). While any patterned or solid-color fabric will work, I like bright, lively colors for this fold. Use medium- to heavyweight cloth napkins, iron them with spray starch before folding and press gently after folding. Place a button, candy, stone, coin or other decorative element where the eye would be on each napkin.

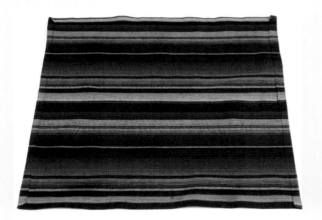

1 Lay the napkin out as a square, with the finished side facing down and the seamed edges facing up.

2 Fold the upper left corner down to the lower right corner, forming a triangle.

3 Turn the triangle so that the widest edge is at the top. Fold the upper edge down to form a 2-inch (5 cm) wide band.

4 Flip the napkin over, keeping the point down.

5 Holding the middle of the upper edge with your right hand, use your left hand to fold the left point down so that the band meets the vertical centerline, leaving a tail at the bottom.

6 Fold the right point down so that the band meets the vertical centerline, leaving a tail at the bottom.

7 Fold the left tail at a 90-degree angle to point out to the left. Fold the right tail at a 90-degree angle to point out to the right. Using an iron, gently press into place.

8 Flip the napkin over. Arrange the fish on a plate, facing right or left. Add a decorative eye, if desired.

#61 Fleur

Arranged in a coffee cup or teacup, this is a lovely fold for serving after-dinner coffee, tea or dessert. Use a slightly smaller napkin that is ironed without starch. Any color or pattern and any fabric weight will work well; I chose a silky purple napkin arranged in a white china coffee cup. For larger latte-style mugs, use a full-size dinner napkin.

1 Lay the napkin out as a square, with the finished side facing down and the seamed edges facing up.

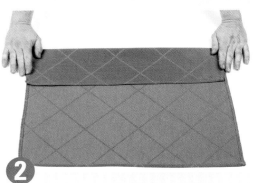

2 Fold the lower edge up to the horizontal centerline of the napkin.

3 Fold the upper edge down to the horizontal centerline.

4 Fold the upper edge down to the lower edge, forming a narrow horizontal rectangle.

5 Fold the right edge over to the left edge, forming a smaller rectangle.

6 Fold the top layer back over to the right, leaving a small overlapped area about three-quarters of the way along the napkin.

7 Fold the right side back over to the left, aligning the right edges.

8 Fold the loose edges in the center of the napkin back over to the right, aligning the left edges. If necessary, fold the end of the right edge back over to the left to align the right edges.

9 Flip the napkin over, arranging the stack of folded edges on the left and the loose end on the right. Fold the right edge over to the left, aligning the right edges.

10 Continue folding accordion-style until napkin is completely folded into a stack.

11 Place napkin in cup with the loose edges facing you. Pull gently from the sides to fan the napkin out.

12 Working with the three folded edges facing you, pull each apart at the top to give the napkin more volume. Arrange a cup at each place with the loose edges facing the center of the table.

#62 Fleur de Lis

There is something elegant and a bit royal about this French-inspired fold, which is why I used a beautiful deep purple napkin. It will work with any color or pattern in any fabric weight. Iron napkins with spray starch before folding. You can lay a finished napkin on each plate or arrange it in a wineglass or water glass.

1 Lay the napkin out as a square, with the finished side facing down and the seamed edges facing up.

2 Fold the upper right corner down to the lower left corner, forming a triangle.

3 Fold the lower right point over to the lower left corner, aligning the lower edges.

4 Fold the upper left point down to the lower left corner, forming a square.

5 Working with the upper left corner, insert your thumbs into the center of the layers and pull the upper layers toward the diagonal centerline, forming a triangle with a 3-inch (7.5 cm) base, with the edges aligned along the diagonal centerline. Smooth flat.

6 Working with the lower right corner, insert your thumbs into the center of the layers and pull the upper layers toward the diagonal centerline, forming a triangle with a 3-inch (7.5 cm) base, with the edges aligned along the diagonal centerline. Smooth flat.

7 Fold the upper left edge under to meet the diagonal centerline, forming a narrower triangle on the upper left side.

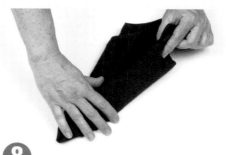

8 Fold the lower right edge under to meet the diagonal centerline, forming a narrower triangle on the lower right side.

9 Rotate the napkin so the point is facing up. Tuck the upper half of the napkin under, forming a flat upper edge.

10 Arrange the napkin with the flat edge facing down.

#**63** Heart

This sweet fold is perfect for Valentine's Day, but it's also welcome anytime you're making a meal for those you love. The Heart fold works well in medium- to heavyweight fabrics with small to medium prints — like the bright pink with white polka dots I used here. It's pretty in solid colors, too. Iron the napkins with spray starch before you begin, and gently press them again after folding to help the heart hold its shape. A delicious cookie place card, a handwritten card or a small wrapped present would be great toppers for this fold.

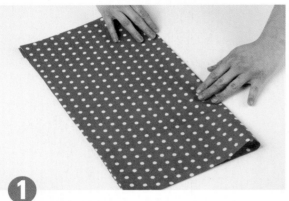

1 Lay the napkin out as a diamond, with the finished side facing down and the seamed edges facing up. Fold the lower left edge up to the upper right edge, forming a rectangle.

2 Fold the lower left edge up to the upper right edge again, forming a narrower rectangle.

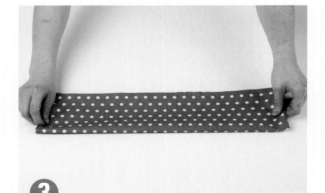

3 Rotate the napkin so that the fold is at the top and the loose edges are at the bottom.

4 Holding the middle of the upper edge with your left hand, use your right hand to fold the right half of the upper edge down to the vertical centerline of the napkin.

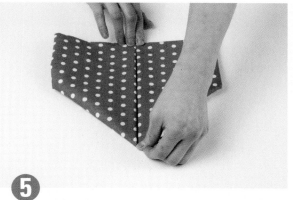

5 Fold the left half of the upper edge down to the vertical centerline of the napkin.

6 Flip the napkin over, keeping the point up and the tails down. Working on the left tail, fold the lower right and left corners in to meet at the vertical centerline of the tail, forming a point.

7 Working on the right tail, fold the lower right and left corners in to meet at the vertical centerline of the tail, forming a point.

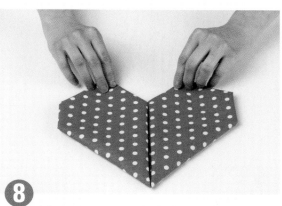

8 Flip the napkin over and arrange a heart at each place with the point facing down.

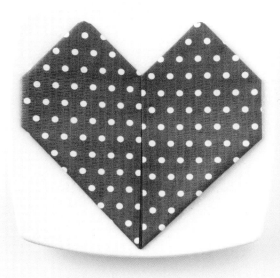

#**64** Herb Pot

This pretty fold works well with smaller napkins in a thicker fabric, such as the ivory and green herb pattern I chose. Iron napkins with spray starch for the best results; after folding, gently press. Tuck a few fresh herb sprigs inside each pot for a lovely scent that complements what you're serving. For a completely different look, use black or orange napkins and candy eyes to turn this herb pot into a Halloween cat.

1 Lay the napkin out as a square, with the finished side facing down and the seamed edges facing up.

2 Fold the upper right corner down to the lower left corner, forming a triangle.

3 Rotate the napkin so that the longest side is at the top. Fold the lower point up to the center of the napkin.

4 Fold the upper edge down to the center to meet the point.

Holding the middle of the upper edge with your left hand, use your right hand to fold the right point over and down to the left, aligning the lower edges of the napkin and leaving a tail on the lower left side.

Fold the left point over and down to the right, aligning the lower edges of the napkin and leaving a tail on the lower right side.

Flip the napkin over and arrange with the flat edge facing down and the points facing up.

#65 High Tower

This fold can be used as a pocket for utensils, set to the left of each plate, or it can be arranged atop each dinner plate. It works with any color or pattern, in any fabric weight; I chose a solid dark blue napkin. Iron napkins with spray starch before folding, and lightly press after folding.

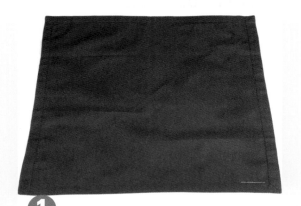

1 Lay the napkin out as a square, with the finished side facing down and the seamed edges facing up.

2 Fold the upper left corner down toward the lower right corner, leaving about 2 inches (5 cm) of the bottom layer showing.

3 Flip the napkin over, arranging it with the longest side at the top.

4 Working with the upper left point, fold the top third of the left side down, aligning the edges on the left side.

5 Working with the upper right point, fold the top third of the right side down, aligning the edges on the right side.

6 Fold the upper edge down about 2 inches (5 cm).

7 Flip the napkin over, keeping the flat edge at the top.

8 Fold the left point one-third of the way over to the right point.

9 Fold the right point over so that the point touches the left edge. Arrange a napkin at each place with the point facing up.

#66 Little Bird

Recreate this pretty fold with any solid or patterned napkin that suits your theme; I chose a blue and white pattern that would be well suited to a brunch, lunch or casual cookout. Light- to medium-weight fabrics work best, as they won't get too thick with the multiple folds required for this design. Starch and press napkins before you begin folding.

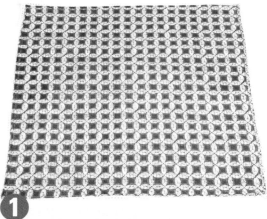

1 Lay the napkin out as a square, with the finished side facing down and the seamed edges facing up.

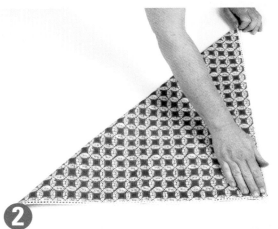

2 Fold the lower right corner up to the upper left corner, forming a triangle.

3 Fold the upper left corner down to the middle of the lower right edge.

4 Holding the middle of the lower right edge with your right hand, use your left hand to fold the lower left point up at an angle toward the right.

5 Fold the right tip over to the left, overlapping the previous fold and aligning all edges along the lower left, forming a point on the lower right side.

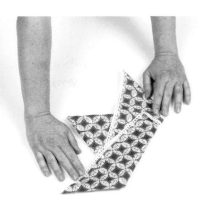

6 Using one-third of the napkin's height, fold the end with two points over toward the lower right point.

7 Fold the lower left point underneath the napkin to meet the upper right point, folding the napkin in half.

8 Fold the lower right point down to form the bird's head. Arrange a bird at each place.

#**67** Lotus

This is a beautiful fold to place between a plate and a bowl. It's also gorgeous arranged in a shallow bowl, where it looks a little like an artichoke. I chose a medium blue napkin, but you can use any color or pattern, in any fabric weight. Iron napkins with spray starch before folding.

1 Lay the napkin out as a square, with the finished side facing down and the seamed edges facing up.

2 Fold the lower left corner in to the center of the napkin.

3 Fold the lower right corner in to the center.

4 Fold the top left and top right corners in to the center, forming a diamond.

5 Fold the bottom point up to the center.

6 Fold the top point down to the center.

7 Fold the left point and right point in to the center, forming a square.

8 Flip the napkin over, keeping it arranged as a square. Fold the lower left and lower right corners in to the center.

10 Holding the center of the diamond steady with your left hand, use your right hand to reach underneath the right point and find the center point beneath it. Gently pull that point out to form a petal.

9 Fold the upper left and upper right corners in to the center, forming a diamond.

11 Holding the center of the diamond steady with your right hand, use your left hand to reach underneath the top point and find the center point beneath it. Gently pull that point out to form a petal.

12 Repeat on the bottom and left points. Holding the center of the diamond steady with your right hand, use your left hand to reach underneath each point and find the center point beneath it. Gently pull each center point out to form a petal.

13 Adjust petals as necessary and arrange a lotus at each place.

#68 Orchid 1

This soft, elegant fold is arranged in a wineglass; alternatively, you could pull the end of the fold through a napkin ring and lay it flat on a dinner plate. Use any fabric weight in any color or pattern you like, tailoring your choice to fit the occasion. I used a yellow patterned napkin. Iron napkins with spray starch before folding, and have one wineglass, water glass or napkin ring per napkin ready before you begin folding.

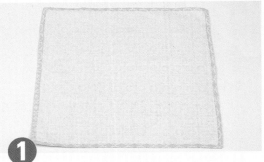

1 Lay the napkin out as a square, with the finished side facing down and the seamed edges facing up.

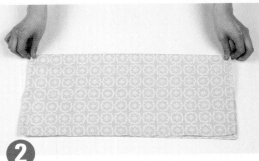

2 Fold the lower edge up to the upper edge, forming a horizontal rectangle.

3 Fold the upper right point down to the middle of the lower edge.

4 Fold the upper left point down to the middle of the lower edge, forming a triangle.

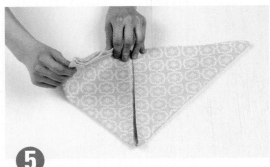

5 Fold the lower right point up to meet the upper point.

6 Fold the lower left point up to meet the upper point, forming a diamond.

7 Working with the right side of the diamond, lift the top layer of the upper point, put your thumbs inside the layers to open them up and fold the top 1 inch (2.5 cm) of the point to the right, forming a petal shape.

9 Pick up the napkin from the bottom third, pinching about 1 inch (2.5 cm) of the bottom edge on each side to meet behind the napkin, with the right and left points still splayed to the sides.

8 Working with the left side of the diamond, lift the top layer of the upper point, put your thumbs inside the layers to open them up and fold the top 1 inch (2.5 cm) of the point to the left, forming a petal shape.

10 Drop the napkin into a wineglass and gently arrange the petals.

#69 Paper Football

Do you remember those paper footballs that bored school kids like to fold — and then throw at each other? This whimsical fold is a grownup version of that, rendered in cloth. Use the Paper Football design for a Super Bowl Party (page 306) or Friends' Game Night (page 302). This fold works in any color or pattern in a medium-weight fabric; I chose a striking chartreuse color here. Press napkins before folding.

1 Lay the napkin out as a square, with the finished side facing down and the seamed edges facing up.

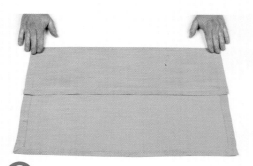

2 Fold the lower edge up toward the upper edge, using one-third the height of the napkin.

3 Fold the upper edge down to the lower edge, forming a horizontal rectangle.

4 Fold the upper right corner down toward the left, forming a point at the lower right corner.

5 Fold the angled right edge up to the upper edge, forming a triangle on top of the napkin.

6 Fold the angled right edge down to the lower edge, forming another triangle.

7 Fold the lower left corner up toward the right, forming a point at the upper left corner.

8 Tuck the upper left point under the top layer of triangle to secure it. Arrange a napkin at each place or on a buffet.

#70 Parrot

Brightly striped fabrics really show off the shape of this napkin fold, but it will work with nearly any color or pattern. I used an aqua, orange, brown and gold striped napkin that gives the fold the tropical look I was after. This fold works best with medium- to heavyweight fabric; iron napkins with spray starch before folding. After folding, gently press the tail for a tailored look or leave it as is for a more casual look.

1 Lay the napkin out as a square, with the finished side facing down and the seamed edges facing up.

2 Fold the lower edge up to the upper edge, forming a horizontal rectangle.

3 Lift the top layer of the upper right corner with your left hand and use your right hand to fold the lower right corner inside the napkin to the vertical centerline.

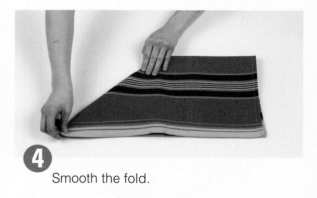

4 Smooth the fold.

5 Lift the top layer of the upper left corner with your right hand and use your left hand to fold the lower left corner inside the napkin to the vertical centerline.

6 Smooth out the large triangle.

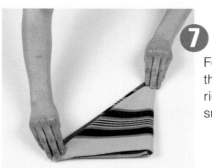

7 Fold the left point of the triangle over to the right point, forming a smaller triangle.

8 Holding the triangle's lowest point with your right hand, use your left hand to fan out the four upper right points.

9 Flip the napkin over so that the points are at the upper left and the folded edge is at the lower right. Working from the folded edge, roll the napkin up about halfway.

10 Flip the napkin over again and arrange the parrot.

#**71** Peacock

Easier than it looks, this fold begins with a simple accordion-style pleat placed in a stemmed glass. The result is an exotic peacock design, with a tail that drapes dramatically down to the table. Heavyweight fabrics ironed with spray starch work best; I chose a dark blue brocade. You can use any color or pattern, but avoid large prints, as they will distract from the visual impact of the finished fold. Have one stemmed wineglass ready for each napkin.

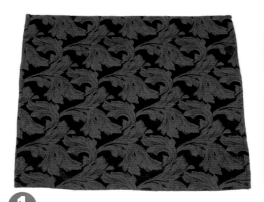

1 Lay the napkin out as a square, with the finished side facing down and the seamed edges facing up.

2 Fold the lower right corner in about 2 inches (5 cm).

3 Fold the same edge under about 2 inches (5 cm).

4 Fold the same edge back over and under, accordion-style, aligning the edges.

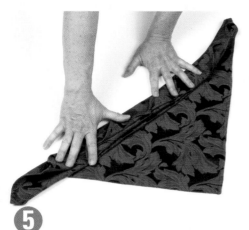

5 Continue folding the napkin accordion-style.

6 When the napkin is completely folded to the upper left corner, pick it up and bend it about one-third from one end, placing the bend in a wineglass.

7 Arrange the short end as the peacock's head and fan out the long end, allowing it to drape down to the table as the peacock's tail.

#**72** Pinwheel

This festive napkin fold enlivens the table for any casual occasion, whether for kids or adults. Solid or patterned napkins of any weight will work well; I chose a blue and white fruit pattern. Iron napkins with spray starch before folding, and gently press after folding.

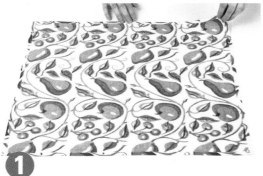

1 Lay the napkin out as a square, with the finished side facing down and the seamed edges facing up.

2 Fold the lower left corner in to the center of the napkin.

3 Fold the lower right corner in to the center.

4 Fold the upper left and upper right corners in to the center, forming a diamond.

5 Rotate the napkin and arrange it as a square. Fold the left edge over to the vertical centerline.

6 Fold the right edge over to the vertical centerline, forming a vertical rectangle.

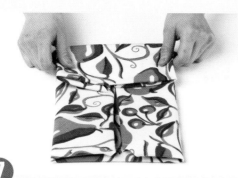

7 Fold the lower edge up to the horizontal centerline.

8 Fold the upper edge down to the horizontal centerline, forming a square.

9 Loosen the two tips from inside the top layer at the left side of the square, gently pulling them out to form a point.

10 Loosen the two tips from inside the top layer at the right side of the square, gently pulling them out to form a point.

11 Fold the upper half of the left point so that it points straight up, perpendicular to its original position.

12 Fold the lower half of the right point so that it points straight down, perpendicular to its original position.

#73 Pointed Pocket

Slip your silverware into this pretty pocket for a beautiful presentation. This fold works for any sit-down occasion, but it's especially nice for the Garden Brunch table setting (page 274). While this fold works well with any color, solids show off its multiple layers better than patterns; I chose a solid bright yellow napkin. Keep in mind, too, that a portion of the napkin's reverse side will be visible in the finished fold. For very finished-looking results, press the fabric both before and after folding.

1 Lay the napkin out as a diamond, with the finished side facing down and the seamed edges facing up. Fold the lower left edge up to the upper right edge, forming a rectangle.

2 Fold the lower right edge up to the upper left edge, forming a diamond.

3 Fold the top layer of the upper point down toward the lower point, leaving ½ inch (1 cm) of the bottom layer showing.

4 Fold the next layer of the upper point down toward the lower point, leaving ½ inch (1 cm) of the previous layer showing.

5 Fold the third layer of the upper point down toward the lower point, leaving ½ inch (1 cm) of the previous layer showing.

6 Flip the napkin over, keeping the same point at the bottom. Fold the left point over toward the right, using one-third the width of the napkin.

7 Fold the right point over to the left edge, overlapping the previous fold.

8 Flip the napkin over and arrange it with the long point down.

#74 Pouf

This soft, festive napkin design is anchored in a wineglass, with a collection of little poufs at the top and no visible folds. You can dress it up by using a silky napkin or make it more causal with a fun print, such as the multicolored floral napkin I used here. This fold works best with unstarched pressed napkins in a lightweight fabric. The smaller the glass you plan to use, the lighter the fabric should be.

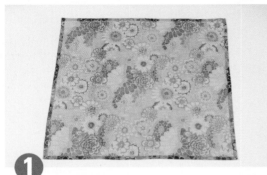

1 Lay the napkin out as a square, with the finished side facing down and the seamed edges facing up.

2 Fold the lower edge up to the upper edge, forming a horizontal rectangle.

3 Fold the right edge over to the left edge, forming a square.

4 Rotate the napkin and arrange it as a diamond, with the loose edges at the top.

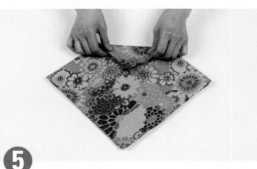

5 Fold the lower point up halfway to the center of the napkin.

6 Fold the right point over to meet the left point.

7 Fold the top layer back over to the right, using about two-thirds the width of the lower edge.

8 Fold the right point back over to the left, aligning the right edge with the layer beneath.

9 Fold the tip of the top layer back over to the right, touching the tip to the right edge.

10 Flip the napkin over, keeping the point up. Fold the right tip over to the left, aligning the right edge with the layers beneath.

11 Fold the left tip back over to the right, aligning the left edge with the layers beneath.

12 Fold the tip of the top layer back over to the left, touching the tip to the left edge.

13 Drop the napkin into a wineglass, with the points up, and gently separate the four top points, bending the middle two away from each other.

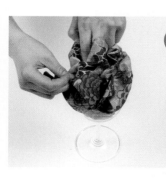

14 Tuck the two right points in toward each other and the two left points in toward each other, puffing each one up as you tuck, to form four small poufs.

#75 Reveal

This fold is designed to show off a double-sided napkin. The finished design is a simple diamond with a small portion peeled back to reveal the napkin's reverse side. I chose a pretty red, green and yellow napkin with a floral design on one side and stripes on the other. Any fabric weight works. Iron napkins with spray starch before folding. After folding, gently press for a tailored look or leave as is for a more casual look.

1 Lay the napkin out as a square, with the finished side facing down and the seamed edges facing up.

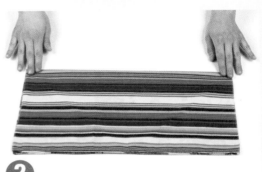

2 Fold the lower edge up to the upper edge, forming a horizontal rectangle.

3 Fold the left edge up to the upper edge.

4 Fold the right edge up to the upper edge, forming a triangle.

5 Flip the napkin over, keeping the same point down.

6 Fold the left point down to the lower point.

7 Fold the right point down to the lower point, forming a diamond.

8 Working with the top layer, pick up the lower left tip and peel back the outermost layer 1 to 2 inches (2.5 to 5 cm) to the left to reveal the fabric on the reverse side. Smooth to flatten.

9 Working with the top layer, pick up the lower right tip and peel back the outermost layer 1 to 2 inches (2.5 to 5 cm) to the right to reveal the fabric on the reverse side. Smooth to flatten. Arrange the napkin with the revealed points up.

#76 Shawl

This napkin fold looks like a shawl wrapped around the shoulders and overlapping in front, making it perfect for a ladies' gathering. If possible, use a double-sided napkin, since both sides will show. I chose a napkin with a yellow and green floral pattern on one side and coordinating stripes on the other. Any fabric weight works with this fold. Iron with spray starch before folding. After folding, gently press for a tailored look or leave as is for a more casual look.

1 Lay the napkin out as a square, with the finished side facing down and the seamed edges facing up.

2 Fold the upper left corner in to the center of the napkin.

3 Fold the newly folded edge over again, taking it just past the center point of the napkin.

4 Flip the napkin over, arranging it with the flat fold at the top. Fold the lower point up to the original center of the napkin.

5 Fold the newly folded lower edge up, taking it just past the point in the center.

6 Fold the left point down and to the right, so that the tail hangs past the lower edge of the napkin with its lower edge parallel to the napkin.

7 Fold the right point down and to the left, placing the right tail on top of the left tail and aligning the lower edges.

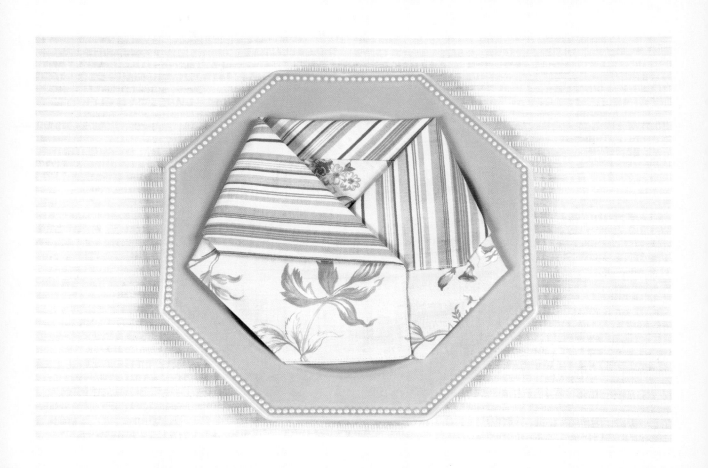

#77 Stairway

With a finished fold that stands upright on the plate, mimicking the ascent of a spiral staircase, this is a dramatically stylish presentation. While any color or pattern will do, be sure to choose a thick, sturdy fabric, such as the brown woven napkin with a subtle border that I used here, and iron napkins with plenty of spray starch before folding. For the crispest results, press the napkin again before rolling it and standing it upright.

1 Lay the napkin out as a square, with the finished side facing down and the seamed edges facing up.

2 Fold the lower edge up to the upper edge, forming a horizontal rectangle.

3 Lift the top layer of the upper right corner with your left hand and use your right hand to fold the lower right corner inside the napkin to the vertical centerline.

4 Lift the top layer of the upper left corner with your right hand and use your left hand to fold the lower left corner inside the napkin to the vertical centerline, forming a triangle.

5 Fold the left side of the triangle over to the right side, forming a smaller triangle. Press all four layers of the points, if desired.

6 Starting at the left side of the triangle, roll up the napkin, keeping it aligned at the upper edge.

7 Continue rolling the napkin almost to the end. Stand the napkin up on the wider end, holding it upright.

8 Fan out the four points at the base of the napkin, allowing it to stand upright and creating a spiral staircase effect.

#78 Straight to the Point

This napkin fold can be arranged flat or standing upright at each place. If you choose the latter presentation, consider tucking a candy, small favor or dinner roll into the center of each. This fold works well with medium- to heavyweight fabrics in any solid or patterned fabric. I chose a colorful floral print with bright teals and pinks on a chartreuse background. If you plan to stand the finished napkins up, it's important to starch the fabric. Either way, iron them before folding.

1 Lay the napkin out as a square, with the finished side facing down and the seamed edges facing up.

2 Fold the lower edge up toward the upper edge, using one-third the height of the napkin.

3 Fold the upper edge down to the lower edge, forming a horizontal rectangle.

4 Holding the middle of the upper edge with your left hand, use your right hand to fold the right half of the upper edge down to the vertical centerline of the napkin.

5 Fold the left half of the upper edge down to the vertical centerline, forming a triangle with two tails hanging below it.

6 Fold the lower edge of the right tail up to meet the base of the triangle.

7 Fold the right tail up again, forming a band along the bottom of the right side of the triangle.

8 Fold the lower edge of the right tail up to meet the base of the triangle. Fold the left tail up again, forming a band along the bottom of the left side of the triangle.

9 Fold the right side over toward the left, using one-third the width of the napkin.

10 Fold the left side over to the right, tucking it behind the top layer to secure it. Arrange a napkin point side up at each place. Alternatively, open up the base and stand the napkin upright.

#**79** A Tisket, a Tasket

This cheerful fold incorporates two napkins; it works best with light-to medium-weight napkins, one a solid color and one patterned. I paired a solid dark pink napkin with a yellow print. Iron napkins with spray starch before folding; after folding, gently press for a tailored look or leave as is for a more casual look. As a finishing touch, tuck a place card, a small party favor or a sprig of herbs into each basket.

1 Lay the solid-color napkin out as a square, with the finished side facing down and the seamed edges facing up. Place the patterned napkin on top as an offset square, with the finished side facing down and the seamed edges facing up, leaving about 1 inch (2.5 cm) of the solid-color napkin showing at the left and upper edges.

2 Fold the lower right corner of the patterned napkin up to the upper left corner of the patterned napkin, forming a triangle atop a square.

3 Fold the lower right corner of the solid-color napkin up toward the upper left corner of both napkins, forming a triangle with three staggered layers showing.

4 Flip the napkins over and arrange with the folded flat edge at the bottom.

5 Holding the middle of the lower edge with your left hand, use your right hand to fold the right point up toward the upper point, forming a vertical centerline.

6 Fold the left point up toward the upper point, forming a diamond.

7 Flip the napkin over, keeping the same point up. Holding the lower point with your left hand, use your right hand to fold the right point over to the vertical centerline.

8 Holding the lower point with your right hand, use your left hand to fold the left point over to the vertical centerline.

9 Using a little less than half the napkin's height, fold the lower point under, creating a flat lower edge.

10 Arrange the napkin with the flat edge down.

#80 Triple Layer

This design gets its name from the three layers that show in the finished fold. To make the most of the presentation, choose a double-sided napkin, such as the green floral with solid red reverse side I used here. Iron napkins with spray starch before folding. After folding, gently press for a tailored look or leave as is for a more casual look.

1 Lay the napkin out as a square, with the finished side facing down and the seamed edges facing up.

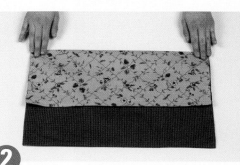

2 Fold the lower edge up toward the upper edge, using one-third the height of the napkin.

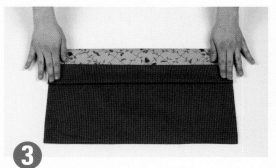

3 Working with the top layer, fold the upper edge halfway down to the lower edge of the napkin.

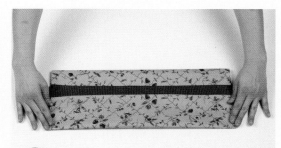

4 Fold the upper edge down enough to just cover the upper fold, forming a horizontal rectangle with three bands.

5 Flip the napkin over, keeping the same edges up and down. Fold the right edge over toward the left, creating a vertical band about 2 inches (5 cm) wide.

6 Fold the band over toward the left again.

7 Fold the band over toward the left a third time.

8 Fold the left edge over toward the right, creating a vertical band about 2 inches (5 cm) wide.

9 Fold the band over toward the right two more times, until the left side either overlaps the right side (as in the photo at left) or meets the right side (as in the photo below).

#81 Tuxedo

This fold offers each guest two napkins, the black for dinner and the white for dessert (or vice versa). The two-tone color scheme features both napkins in crisp diagonal stripes. While the black and white combination is formal, this design is very flexible, working well with any two colors — or a solid color with a coordinated patterned napkin. Iron all napkins with spray starch before folding; after folding, gently press.

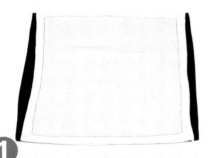

1 Lay the first napkin out as a square, with the finished side facing down and the seamed edges facing up. Lay the second napkin out as a square on top of the first napkin, with the finished side facing down and the seamed edges facing up.

2 Holding both lower edges together, fold the lower edges up to the upper edges, forming a horizontal rectangle.

3 Fold the right edge over to the left edge, forming a square.

4 Working with the top layer only, fold the upper left corner back about 1 inch (2.5 cm).

5 Fold that corner down again, repeating the fold about three more times until the top napkin forms a band that divides the square diagonally.

6 Working with the top layer of the upper left corner, tuck the corner under itself just far enough to leave a 1-inch (2.5 cm) band of napkin showing parallel to the first band.

7 Working with the next three layers of the upper left corner, fold the corners over and tuck them under the previous band far enough to leave another 1-inch (2.5 cm) band of napkin showing parallel to the first and second bands.

8 Flip the napkin over, keeping the same edges up and down. Fold the right edge over toward the left edge, forming a 2-inch (5 cm) wide vertical band.

9 Fold the left edge almost to the right edge, overlapping the previous fold.

10 Flip the napkin over.

#82 Two-Headed Fish

To me, this design looks a little like a two-headed fish — thus the name — but given that it's a pretty abstract representation, you can use it for nearly any occasion. It works best with a medium- to heavyweight fabric, in any color or pattern; I used a bright yellow and white fruit pattern. Iron napkins with spray starch before folding, and gently press them after folding.

1 Lay the napkin out as a square, with the finished side facing down and the seamed edges facing up.

2 Fold the lower left corner in to the center of the napkin.

3 Fold the lower right corner in to the center.

4 Fold the upper right and upper left corners in to the center, forming a diamond.

5 Holding the napkin by the middle of the upper left and lower right sides, carefully pick it up and tuck the upper right side under the lower left side.

6 Arrange the napkin as a horizontal rectangle, with the middle triangle pointing up.

7 Fold the left edge over to the right edge, forming a square.

8 Fold the top layer of the lower right corner up to the upper left corner.

9 Fold the top layer of the upper left corner under itself twice to form a narrow band.

10 Fold the top layer of the lower right corner under itself twice to form a narrow band.

11 Flip the napkin over, arranging it as a diamond with a vertical crease. Fold the left and right points in to meet at the center.

12 Flip the napkin back over and arrange it on a plate.

#**83** Viking

This napkin fold gets its name from its resemblance to a horned Viking helmet. I played up the connection by using a fabric with a Nordic-style pattern, in natural shades of rust, brown and cream. Choose medium-weight napkins in any color or pattern, and starch the napkins before ironing them if you plan to stand the finished folds upright.

1 Lay the napkin out as a diamond, with the finished side facing down and the seamed edges facing up.

2 Fold the upper point down to the lower point, forming a triangle.

3 Fold the right point down to the lower point.

4 Fold the left point down to the lower point, forming a diamond.

5 Fold the top layer of the lower left tip up to the upper tip, forming a small triangle on the upper left half of the diamond.

6 Fold the top layer of the lower right tip up to the upper tip, forming a small triangle on the upper right half of the diamond.

7 Working with the small triangle at the upper left, fold the upper tip down toward the left, forming a small triangle with a tip that hangs past the upper left edge of the diamond.

8 Working with the small triangle at the upper right, fold the upper tip down toward the right, forming a small triangle with a tip that hangs past the upper right edge of the diamond.

9 Fold the lower point of the diamond up toward the upper point, leaving about 2 inches (5 cm) of the bottom layer showing.

10 Flip the napkin over, keeping the same point at the top.

11 Fold the lower edge about 1 inch (2.5 cm) underneath the napkin, forming a band.

12 Fold the right tip over toward the left, using about one-third the width of the napkin.

13 Fold the left tip over toward the right, tucking it under the top layer of the previous fold to secure it.

14 Flip the napkin over and arrange it with the flat edge down. Alternatively, open up the base and stand the napkin upright.

#84 Wave

Use this fold as a pretty pocket for utensils or a place card; you can place each utensil behind a different wave, if you like. I used a medium blue napkin here to play up the watery look, but it works well with any color or pattern in any fabric weight. Iron napkins with spray starch before folding, and lightly press after folding.

1 Lay the napkin out as a square, with the finished side facing down and the seamed edges facing up.

2 Fold the lower edge up to the upper edge, forming a horizontal rectangle.

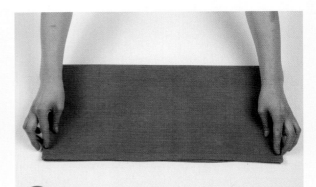

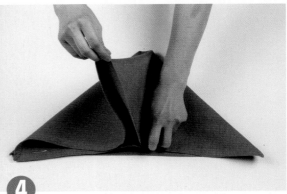

3 Lift the top layer of the upper right corner with your left hand and use your right hand to fold the lower right corner inside the napkin to the vertical centerline.

4 Lift the top layer of the upper left corner with your right hand and use your left hand to fold the lower left corner inside the napkin to the vertical centerline, forming a triangle.

5 Fold the left point of the triangle over to the right point, forming a smaller triangle.

6 Holding the bottom point steady with your right hand, use your left hand to fan out four layers of points at the upper right side.

7 Tuck the bottom point under to meet the upper left corner, aligning the left edges.

8 Arrange the napkin vertically. For placing napkin over utensils as in the picture below, simply twist end under.

#85 Whale's Tail

For each finished fold, you'll need to have one water glass or wineglass ready. A solid white napkin would dress this design up for a more formal party. A bright multicolored stripe, such as the yellow, green, tan and red napkin I used here, makes this a fun fold for the Mexican Fiesta on page 322. Use lightly starched and pressed medium-weight cloth napkins.

1 Lay the napkin out as a square, with the finished side facing down and the seamed edges facing up.

2 Fold the upper edge down to the lower edge, forming a horizontal rectangle.

3 Fold the right edge over to the left edge, forming a square.

4 Fold the upper right corner in toward the center, using about 1½ inches (4 cm) of fabric to form a small triangle.

5 Fold triangle under napkin and then over napkin again, accordion-style.

6 Make two more accordion folds in the napkin, leaving the lower left corner of the napkin unfolded.

7 Turn the napkin so that the accordion folds are at the lower edge and pick up the napkin by the accordion folds, folding it in half.

8 Drop the napkin into a glass.

#86 Wide Collar

This versatile fold works well with solid-color or patterned napkins, and can go formal or casual. I chose a solid-color napkin with a decorative border, which shows up nicely in the finished fold. Light- to medium-weight napkins work best. Begin this fold with pressed starched napkins and press the finished fold again, if necessary, to keep the two sides of the collar lying flat. Tuck a flower, place card or small favor inside each finished napkin, if you like.

1 Lay the napkin out as a square, with the finished side facing down and the seamed edges facing up.

2 Fold the lower right corner up to the upper left corner, forming a triangle.

3 Fold the lower left point up to the upper left corner, aligning the left edges.

4 Fold the upper right point over to the upper left corner, forming a square.

5 Flip the napkin over, arranging it with the loose edges at the lower right corner.

6 Fold the lower right corner up to the upper left corner, forming a triangle.

7 Fold the lower left point over toward the upper right point, using about one-third the length of the diagonal and aligning the edges at the lower right.

8 Fold the upper right point down toward the lower left edge, tucking it underneath the top layer of the previous fold.

9 Arrange the napkin with the point facing down. Working with the top layer of the point, fold the left half out to the left and the right half out to the right. Press the points to keep them flat, if necessary.

10 Arrange the napkin with the point facing up.

#87 Wings

This pretty upright napkin fold looks ready for takeoff, with a wing balancing it on either side. You can make a small version using luncheon napkins or a larger version using dinner napkins. Use fabric in any weight and in any color or pattern; I chose a dark gold fringed napkin. Iron napkins with spray starch before folding.

1 Lay the napkin out as a diamond, with the finished side facing down and the seamed edges facing up.

2 Fold the bottom point up to the top point, forming a triangle.

3 Fold the left point up to the upper point.

4 Fold the right point up to the upper point, forming a diamond.

5 Fold the lower point up toward the upper point, leaving about 1 inch (2.5 cm) of the bottom layer showing.

6 Working with the top layer, fold the upper point down to the lower edge.

7 Flip the napkin over, arranging it with the flat fold at the bottom.

8 Fold the left point over to the right, using about one-third the width of the napkin and aligning the lower edges.

9 Fold the right point over to the left, tucking it into the pocket at the left.

10 Stand the napkin fold up, gently squeezing the sides together to form a circular base. Fold the left point down.

11 Fold the right point down.

Advanced Napkin Folds

#88 Aloha Shirt

To play up the fun, casual look of this fold, choose a tropical-looking fabric, like the dark yellow and orange patterned napkin I used here. This fold works well with fabrics of any weight, color or pattern — select something that suits your occasion, from team colors to Hawaiian prints. Iron napkins with spray starch before folding, and gently press again after folding to help napkins keep their shape (this will be particularly necessary with smaller or thicker napkins).

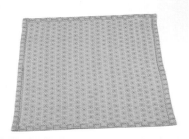

1 Lay the napkin out as a square, with the finished side facing down and the seamed edges facing up.

2 Fold the left edge to the vertical centerline of the napkin

3 Fold the right edge to the vertical centerline.

4 Fold the lower edge under about 1 inch (2.5 cm).

5 Fold the lower left corner in to touch the vertical centerline, creating a narrow triangle on the left that will represent half of the shirt's collar.

6 Fold the lower right corner in to touch the vertical centerline, creating a narrow triangle on the right that will represent the other half of the shirt's collar.

7 Holding the center of the napkin steady with your right hand, use your left hand to pick up the top layer at the upper left and fold the loose corner back, forming a narrow triangle on the left.

8 Holding the center of the napkin steady with your left hand, use your right hand to pick up the top layer at the upper right and fold the loose corner back, forming a narrow triangle on the right.

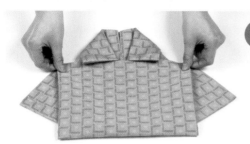

9 Fold the upper edge down to the collar, tucking the edge beneath both tips of the collar.

#89 Bamboo

This sweet little fold is suitable for smaller dishes, so perch it atop salad or dessert plates. Use a thicker napkin, as lightweight fabric won't give you the body you need. Any color or pattern will work; I chose a napkin with a yellow background and a light blue toile pattern. Press napkins with spray starch before folding.

1 Lay the napkin out as a square, with the finished side facing down and the seamed edges facing up.

2 Fold the lower edge up toward the upper edge, using one-third the height of the napkin.

3 Fold the upper edge down to the lower edge, forming a horizontal rectangle.

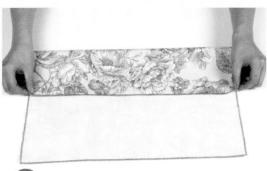

4 Holding the middle of the lower edge with your right hand, use your left hand to fold the left half of the lower edge up to the vertical centerline of the napkin.

5 Fold the right half of the lower edge up to the vertical centerline, forming a triangle with two tails rising above it.

6 Fold the upper edge of the left tail down, aligning the top of the fold with the layer beneath it.

7 Fold the upper edge of the right tail down, aligning the top of the fold with the layer beneath it.

8 Rotate the napkin so that the point faces right. Fold the lower half up over the upper half.

9 Lift the top layer of the upper edge.

10 Tuck the upper edge of the top layer under into the fold.

11 Tuck the upper edge of the bottom layer over into the fold.

12 Stand the napkin up vertically on the flat base, holding the layers together.

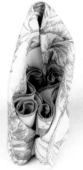

13 Arrange the napkin fold with the tall side at the back, exposing the inner layers.

#90 Bird of Paradise

This striking fold is well worth the effort. To mimic the bright hues of the tropical flower with this name, choose a napkin with at least some orange in it, like this wavy orange, brown, pink and gold striped pattern. With this many folds, softer fabrics work better than thick, stiff fabrics. Press but don't starch the napkins before folding. For the final presentation, you can place this napkin upright or flat on each plate; it looks great either way.

1 Lay the napkin out as a square, with the finished side facing down and the seamed edges facing up.

2 Fold the lower edge up to the upper edge, forming a horizontal rectangle.

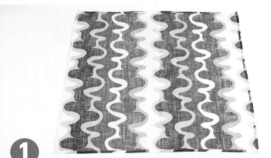

3 Fold the left edge over to the right edge, forming a square.

4 Rotate the square to make a diamond, with the folded edge at the lower left and the loose points at the top. Fold the upper point down to the lower point, forming a triangle.

5 Holding the lower point with your right hand, use your left hand to fold the left point up to the vertical centerline of the napkin.

6 Holding the lower point with your left hand, use your right hand to fold the right point up to the vertical centerline, forming a kite shape.

7 Tuck the top of the kite under, forming a triangle.

8 Rotate the napkin 90 degrees to make an arrow pointing to the left. Bring the upper and lower points closer together underneath the napkin to prop it up.

9 Holding the upper and lower points loosely together with your right hand, use your left hand to gently pull up one layer at a time from the left point, using the four top layers to create a petal-like effect.

#91 Clamshell

The key to this design holding its shape is using a heavyweight fabric ironed well with lots of spray starch. I chose a solid dark blue napkin, but any color or pattern will work as long as the fabric is stiff enough. The effort is well worth it for the showy double fan that stands upright at each place. This fold makes a great first impression.

1 Lay the napkin out as a square, with the finished side facing down and the seamed edges facing up.

2 Fold the lower edge up to the horizontal centerline of the napkin.

3 Fold the upper edge down to the horizontal centerline.

4 Fold the lower edge up to the upper edge, forming a thin horizontal rectangle.

5 Fold the left edge over to the right edge.

6 Holding the left edge in place with your left hand, use your right hand to fold the top layer of the right edge back over to the left, leaving about 1 inch (2.5 cm) of the left edge closed.

7 Fold the left edge back over toward the right edge, aligning the folds at the left.

8 Continue folding the top layer, accordion-style, until you reach the end.

9 Flip the napkin over, arranging it with the stack of folds on the right. Fold the left edge over to the right, aligning the folds at the left.

10 Continue folding the top layer, accordion-style, until you reach the end.

11 Stand the napkin up on one short edge, with the side exposing more layers up.

12 Fan out the edges of the napkin, pulling apart the two layers at each fold to make diamond-like designs visible from above the napkin.

13 Place the base of the napkin on the table and let it fan out to the sides.

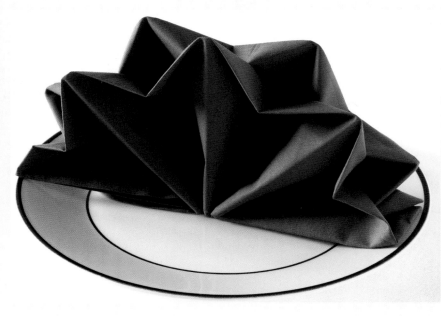

#92 Dutch Baby

This cute little fold looks most elegant when done with a white napkin (as on the bottom of page 211), but it will work in any color or pattern. Here, I chose a solid blue fabric. Because of the many layers of folds, light- to medium-weight fabrics work best. Iron napkins with spray starch before folding.

1 Lay the napkin out as a square, with the finished side facing down and the seamed edges facing up.

2 Fold the lower edge up toward the upper edge, using one-third the height of the napkin.

3 Fold the upper edge down to the lower edge, forming a horizontal rectangle.

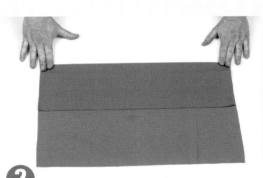

4 Fold the right edge to the vertical centerline of the napkin.

5 Fold the left edge to the vertical centerline.

6 Fold the right half of the lower edge up to the vertical centerline.

7 Fold the lower left edge up to the vertical centerline, forming a downward-pointing arrow.

8 Flip the napkin over, keeping the point down.

9 Fold the flat right edge of the arrow over to the left and down so that what was the upper right edge of the arrow now forms a horizontal line across the lower third of the napkin.

10 Fold the flat left edge of the arrow over to the right and down, overlapping the previous fold, so that what was the upper left edge of the arrow now forms a horizontal line across the lower third of the napkin. Tuck the corner under the top layer of the previous fold to secure it.

11 Flip the napkin over, arranging it with the wider end down. Open up the inside of the napkin into a rounded base.

12 Stand the napkin upright on its base.

#93 Elf Boot

This fanciful design is perfect for a Christmastime table when made with a red or green napkin; otherwise, any color or pattern will work well. Use a medium-weight fabric — you want some heft for stability but not so much that the napkin gets too thick with multiple folds — and lightly starch and press napkins before folding. Arrange a finished boot atop each plate, with a Christmas ornament, perhaps. The Elf Boot fold could also be used as a fairy slipper for a party with a Midsummer Night's Dream theme.

1 Lay the napkin out as a square, with the finished side facing down and the seamed edges facing up.

2 Fold the upper edge down to the lower edge.

3 Fold the upper edge down to the lower edge again, forming a narrow horizontal rectangle.

4 Holding the middle of the upper edge with your left hand, use your right hand to fold the right half of the upper edge down to the vertical centerline.

5 Fold the left half of the upper edge down to the vertical centerline.

6 Fold the upper right edge down to the vertical centerline.

7 Fold the upper left edge down to the vertical centerline.

8 Fold the left half of the napkin over the right half.

9 Flip the napkin over, keeping the same point at the top.

10 Fold the top layer of the lower edge over to the right, perpendicular to the napkin.

11 Fold the lower right corner up to the left edge, forming a small triangle.

12 Fold the lower point up, tucking it underneath the upper triangle to secure it.

13 The result will be a boot shape.

14 Stand the boot up on its base, with the toe pointing away from you.

15 Insert your thumbs inside the upper layers and fold them down over the boot. Arrange a finished boot at each place.

#94 Hummingbird

This challenging yet fun fold can be made with nearly any type of napkin: fabric weight doesn't matter, nor does the pattern. I chose a solid deep green napkin here; another example of the Hummingbird fold appears at the bottom of page 215, where I used a silky gray organza fabric. Iron napkins with spray starch before folding, then press again after folding to help them hold the shape.

1 Lay the napkin out as a diamond, with the finished side facing down and the seamed edges facing up.

2 Fold the right point in toward the lower middle of the napkin until the left edge creates a vertical centerline.

3 Fold the left point in toward the lower middle of the napkin until the right edge meets the vertical centerline, forming a kite shape.

4 Fold the bottom point up, forming a large triangle with a smaller triangle at the base.

5 Fold the lower edge up far enough to just cover the top point of the smaller triangle.

6 Fold the right edge over to the left edge.

7 Fold the top layer of the lower left corner up in a small triangle, aligning the upper left edges.

8 Flip the napkin over. Fold the lower right corner up in a small triangle, aligning the upper edges, forming the tail. Press gently.

9 Working with the longest point, fold it under about halfway up the napkin, extending the tip out in the opposite direction from the tail.

10 Using the top third of the same point, gently lift the point and open it slightly to work with a flat triangle.

11 Fold the point down inside the fold about 2 inches (5 cm), then back up, extending it out about 1 inch (2.5 cm). Fold the point closed, forming the hummingbird's head.

12 Flip the napkin over and spread the tail points apart slightly.

#95 Luna Moth

Use this design for a garden party — or anytime you want a fold that looks like it fluttered in for the occasion. It works well with any color or pattern, but be sure to use a medium-weight fabric ironed with lots of spray starch so that it holds its shape. I chose a gold and brown floral napkin, which makes the fold look like a butterfly. Press the ends of the wings after folding.

1 Lay the napkin out as a square, with the finished side facing down and the seamed edges facing up.

2  Fold the lower edge up to the upper edge, forming a horizontal rectangle.

3  Fold the right edge up to the upper edge.

4 Fold the left edge up to the upper edge, forming a triangle.

5  Flip the napkin over, keeping the same point down. Holding the lower point with your left hand, use your right hand to fold the lower right edge over to the vertical centerline, with the point extending above the napkin at the upper right.

6  Holding the lower point with your right hand, use your left hand to fold the lower left edge over to the vertical centerline, with the point extending above the napkin at the upper left, forming a kite shape.

7 Reach under the right half of the kite and pull the upper right corner from the middle of the kite out to the right.

8 Reach under the left half and pull the upper left corner from the middle out to the left, forming a diamond.

9 Flip the napkin over, keeping the same points up and down.

10 Fold the lower point up to the center of the diamond, then fold the lower edge up again, forming a triangle.

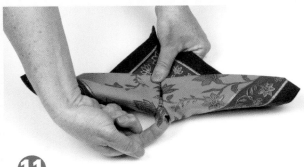

11 Reaching into the center of the base between the left and right sides, pull out the band slightly to separate the wings.

12 Separate the top points slightly and push the left and right sides together at the lower edge to elevate the center, forming a moth.

#96 Orchid 2

Use a water glass or wineglass to hold this flower-inspired napkin fold. While any fabric weight in any color or pattern will work, white fabric or silky solids lend an elegant look; I chose a deep maroon hue. This fold has softer, less visible lines than the Orchid 1 design (page 160), making it more flowing. Iron napkins with a little spray starch before folding. Have one glass ready for each napkin.

1 Lay the napkin out as a diamond, with the finished side facing down and the seamed edges facing up.

2 Fold the lower point up to the upper point, forming a triangle.

3 Fold the right point up to the upper point.

4 Fold the left point up to the upper point, forming a diamond.

5 Fold the lower right edge underneath the diamond to the vertical centerline.

6 Fold the lower left edge underneath the diamond to the vertical centerline.

7 Fold the lower point up to just below the upper point.

8 Bend the left and right sides back enough to fit the bottom of the napkin fold into a glass.

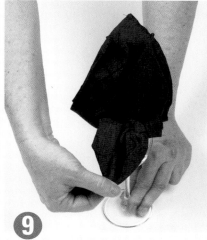

9 Bend the front layer forward to create a petal.

10 Bend the two points behind the front layer to either side, arranging them and the remaining top point into petals.

#97 Rabbit

This cute rabbit will look like it hopped onto your table just for the party. Children and adults alike will appreciate its fun form, and will be reluctant to unfold it for its intended use. I used a cheerful cherry print, but it would be precious in any solid pastel color for a springtime party. This fold works best with a large thin napkin, such as a bandana, as the many folds stack up quickly.

1 Lay the napkin out as a square, with the finished side facing down and the seamed edges facing up.

2 Fold the upper edge down to the lower edge.

3 Fold the upper edge down to the lower edge again, forming a narrow horizontal rectangle.

4 Holding the middle of the upper edge with your left hand, use your right hand to fold the right half of the upper edge down to the vertical centerline.

5 Fold the left half of the upper edge down to the vertical centerline.

6 Fold the lower right corner up to the center of the napkin.

7 Fold the lower left corner up to the center of the napkin, forming a diamond.

8 Fold the lower right edge to the vertical centerline.

9 Fold the lower left edge to the vertical centerline, forming a kite shape.

10 Flip the napkin over, keeping the same point up. Fold the upper point down, forming a triangle.

11 Flip the napkin over again, keeping the same flat edge at the top.

12 Fold the right point over toward the left, using about one-third the width of the napkin.

13 Fold the left point over toward the right, tucking it underneath the top layer of the previous fold.

14 Turn the napkin over and open up the folds of the two top points, forming ears.

15 Arrange a rabbit standing upright at each place.

#98 Swan

This fold works best with a thin fabric, but it needs to be stiff, too, so use plenty of starch and iron napkins before you begin folding. Choose a solid color so the layers of folds won't be obscured by a busy pattern. I used a light green napkin here, but white would be pretty, too. A classic fancy fold the likes of which you'd see on a cruise ship or in an old-school restaurant, the Swan design is great to pull out when you really want to impress. It's fun for the Girls' Night In table setting (page 300), because ladies always appreciate such details.

1 Lay the napkin out as a square, with the finished side facing down and the seamed edges facing up.

2 Fold the upper edge down to the lower edge.

3 Fold the right edge over to the left edge, forming a square.

4 Arrange the square as a diamond, with the loose edges at the top. Holding the lower point with your left hand, use your right hand to fold the lower right edge over to the vertical centerline.

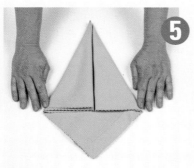

5 Holding the lower point with your right hand, use your left hand to fold the lower left edge over to the vertical centerline, forming a kite shape.

6 Flip the napkin over, keeping the same point up. Holding the lower point with your left hand, use your right hand to fold the lower right edge over to the vertical centerline.

7 Holding the lower point with your right hand, use your left hand to fold the lower left edge over to the vertical centerline.

8 Fold the lower point up to the upper point.

9 Fold the left and right sides of the napkin together underneath the napkin.

10 Stand the fold upright on its base.

11 Fold the narrower point over, forming the swan's head.

12 Working with the wider point, one layer at a time, separate the four layers, forming the swan's tail feathers.

13 Arrange a swan at each place, supported by its tail feathers.

#99 Tropics

You'll need two napkins for this fold, preferably contrasting ones. Try a solid-color napkin and a patterned one for a striking presentation. To play up the tropical look I wanted, I chose a solid magenta napkin and a patterned gold napkin. Iron napkins with generous amounts of spray starch before folding to help them hold their shape when arranged upright. This fold needs to be placed in a glass, so have one wineglass per napkin fold ready before you begin folding.

1 Lay the solid-color napkin out as a diamond, with the finished side facing down and the seamed edges facing up. Place the patterned napkin on top, with the finished side facing down and the seamed edges facing up, arranging it slightly lower than the solid-color napkin so that a bit of the solid-color napkin shows at the top of the diamond.

2 Fold the lower point of the patterned diamond up to the upper point of the patterned diamond, forming a patterned triangle atop a solid-color diamond.

3 Fold the lower point of the solid-color diamond up to just below the upper point of the patterned triangle, forming a triangle with three top points showing.

4 Holding the middle of the lower edge with your left hand, use your right hand to fold the right point up to the upper point.

5 Fold the left point up to the upper point, forming a diamond.

6 Fold the left edge of the right triangle down to the lower right edge, aligning the edges and leaving a tip extending to the right of the diamond.

7 Fold the right edge of the left triangle down to the lower left edge, aligning the edges and leaving a tip extending to the left of the diamond.

8 Flip the napkin fold over, keeping the same point down.

9 Fold the right half over to the left half, forming an arrow.

10 Working with the left side of the arrow, fold the top two layers over to the right side, leaving only solid napkin showing and maintaining the arrow shape.

11 Flip the napkin fold over, arranging it with the arrow pointing down.

12 Fold the right side of the arrow over the left side.

13 Tuck the lower tip up inside the napkin fold, using about one-third the length of the napkin.

14 Drop the bottom of the fold into a wineglass.

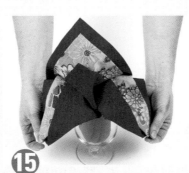

15 Gently separate and arrange the napkin fold's three points.

#100 Weave

Use this intricate fold for the Pacific Northwest Coast table setting (page 314), in cool oceanic shades of teal or blue, or a crisp white — or use it anytime you want to show off your advanced napkin folding skills. A solid-color fabric will highlight the many interlocking layers best. Starch and press the napkins before you begin folding, and lightly press the finished fold for crisp results.

1 Lay the napkin out as a square, with the finished side facing down and the seamed edges facing up. Fold the lower edge up about 1 inch (2.5 cm), forming a band.

2 Holding the edges of the band and lifting it, form another band of the same height above the first one.

3 Holding the edges of both bands and lifting, reposition the bands higher on the napkin, forming another band of equal height below them.

4 Holding the edges of the three bands and lifting, reposition the bands higher on the napkin, forming another band of equal height above them.

5 Holding the edges of the four bands, lift the napkin and let the upper edge fall down underneath, so that it hangs down below the bands.

6 Tuck the loose edge under, leaving just enough showing at the lower edge to form the fifth band.

7 Smooth the bands.

8 Flip the napkin over, keeping the same edges at top and bottom.

9 Holding the middle 2 inches (5 cm) of the lower edge in place with your left hand, use your right hand to fold the right edge toward the upper left.

10 Fold the left edge toward the upper right, partially overlapping the right side.

11 Lifting all layers on the left side, top the innermost layer on the right side with the innermost layer of the left side.

12 Continue interweaving layers with the remaining three inside flaps.

13 Smooth the folds.

14 Flip the napkin over, keeping the same flat edge down. Fold the lower right edge over about 1 inch (2.5 cm), forming a band.

15 Fold the lower left edge over about 1 inch (2.5 cm), forming a band. Flip the napkin over again and arrange it with the narrow end at the top.

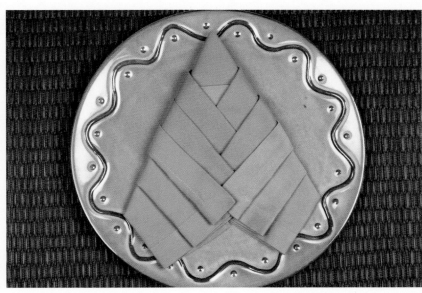

2

Table Settings

Table Settings 101

A table setting that incorporates your prettily folded napkins invites your guests to share in the spirit of your party. Whether the party is elegant or casual, fun or romantic, a picnic or a late-night dinner, the table setting is the stage it is built around.

In this chapter, you'll learn how to purchase, use and care for your linens (check out my helpful tablecloth sizing guide on page 232). Think you don't have enough china, silverware or glassware for your entertaining needs? I'll tell you how to mix and match what you have, and how to borrow or rent what you don't have, to make the most of your table settings. I'll also show you how to create easy and inexpensive centerpieces, inventive place cards and invitations and fun party favors. I've even included ideas for fabulous host/hostess gifts, for those times when you're on the other side of the party experience. And my tips on party etiquette for the 21st century will ensure that you're always a gracious host or hostess or a sought-after guest.

Need to know how to set a formal table? Need to know how to arrange a buffet for the best party flow? Read on.

Tablecloths

Linens can instantly give your tabletop a completely new look. It's typically much less expensive to buy a new tablecloth to fit your party theme than it is to purchase alternative sets of china or flatware, so linens are a great way to mix up the look for less. While a white linen tablecloth is customary for formal entertaining, for most parties the quality of your linens doesn't matter quite as much as what you do with them. Every host should have a set of neutral table linens in white, cream or tan; these will serve as a great foundation for more festive additions, such as a colorful table runner that coordinates with the theme.

Tablecloth or Placemats?

For a large, formal meal, a tablecloth is a better choice than placemats: it provides a single, usually simple backdrop for the meal — an uncluttered look that gives the scene an elegance placemats can't achieve. Placemats, on the other hand, are easier to wash and iron, and they add a coziness to the table that's nice for smaller, less formal gatherings.

That said, for anything-goes modern entertaining, the only

set rule is not to use both placemats and a tablecloth at the same time. If you want to protect your tablecloth from sloshes and spills, invest in a set of chargers — large, decorative plates placed under the dinner plates. They're available at any home goods store, they're inexpensive but elegant, and they'll catch most drips from around each dinner plate. If your table is especially attractive, you might want to use only chargers, instead of mats or a cloth, for a streamlined look that shows off more of the tabletop.

Selecting the Right Tablecloth

When you're shopping for a tablecloth, and they're all folded up into neat little packages, it's hard to imagine how it will look on your table at home. Since tablecloths come in square, rectangular, round and oval, the shape is a natural place to start — keeping in mind, of course, that your round table is oval when the leaf is in place.

Before you shop, measure your table fully extended, assuming that's how you will be using it. Next, add to your table's dimensions the overhang — or the distance between the tabletop and the hem of the tablecloth — you will want on each side. How much overhang you need depends on how pretty or utilitarian your table is and on the formality of the event. In general, a longer overhang makes the table look more luxurious than a shorter one. For a seated dinner, an overhang of 10 to 15 inches (25 to 35 cm) on all sides is standard, hanging neatly to diners' laps. (See the chart on page 232 for help choosing a tablecloth with a standard overhang for your table.) For parties where people will be standing, like buffets or cocktail parties, the overhang can be longer. And if you're using rented tables with unsightly metal legs, the overhang should be floor-length.

As with all table linens, it makes sense to begin by purchasing an ample 100% cotton tablecloth in a light neutral color. Such a tablecloth will make a great background for both formal and fun table settings and can be used year-round, working just as well for Thanksgiving dinner as for a Fourth of July barbecue. When

Silence Cloth

A thick layer of fabric placed underneath the tablecloth softens the sound of dishes being set down and gives the tablecloth itself a more sumptuous look. If your table came with a custom pad, consider yourself lucky and simply use that. Otherwise, you can fashion your own silence cloth by cutting a fabric such as thick felt to fit your table. I've even known a hostess to use a large terrycloth towel or two. While a silence cloth is definitely optional, it's handy for masking an ill-fitting table leaf or minimizing noise in a space that tends to echo.

adding to your tablecloth collection, it's fun to have one or two that help convey your sense of style more colorfully while providing an attractive backdrop for the china, flatware and glassware you own. Some party-givers will get great mileage out of a bright Provence-inspired tablecloth that can be used on the patio table as easily as the dining room table. Others will enjoy a solid tablecloth in a deeper color that coordinates with their china.

If you have inherited tablecloths that don't fit your table, consider using them anyway. You can layer smaller tablecloths over larger ones, bringing sweet (or funky) vintage style to the table. You've likely seen a smaller square tablecloth used atop a larger round one, for instance. Relatives will delight in seeing old family linens repurposed, and even friends who don't know the linens' history will find such tables more personal and unique than those with only perfectly sized, coordinated pieces.

Tablecloth Sizing

Round Tables		
Diameter of Table	**Guests**	**Tablecloth Size**
36 to 48 inches (90 to 120 cm)	4	60 inches (150 cm)
46 to 58 inches (115 to 145 cm)	6	70 inches (175 cm)
64 to 76 inches (160 to 190 cm)	8 to 10	90 inches (225 cm)
Rectangular Tables		
Length and Width of Table	**Guests**	**Tablecloth Size**
36 x 78 inches to 48 x 90 inches (90 x 195 cm to 120 x 225 cm)	6 to 10	60 x 102 inches (150 x 255 cm)
36 x 96 inches to 48 x 108 inches (90 x 240 cm to 120 x 270 cm)	8 to 12	60 x 120 inches (150 x 300 cm)
Square Tables		
Dimensions of Table	**Guests**	**Tablecloth Size**
28 x 28 inches to 40 x 40 inches (70 x 70 cm to 100 x 100 cm)	4	60 x 60 inches (150 x 150 cm)
Oval Tables		
Length and Width	**Guests**	**Tablecloth Size**
28 x 46 inches to 40 x 58 inches (70 x 115 cm to 100 x 145 cm)	4 to 6	52 x 70 inches (130 x 175 cm)
36 x 58 inches to 48 x 70 inches (90 x 145 cm to 120 x 175 cm)	6 to 8	60 x 84 inches (150 x 210 cm)
36 x 78 inches to 48 x 90 inches (90 x 195 cm to 120 x 225 cm)	8 to 10	60 x 102 inches (150 x 255 cm)
36 x 96 inches to 48 x 108 inches (90 x 240 cm to 120 x 270 cm)	12 to 14	60 x 120 inches (150 x 300 cm)

Caring for Your Linens

Care for your tablecloths and cloth napkins properly and they can last for decades. If you've ever looked through an older relative's linens or come across vintage linens at an estate sale, you've likely noticed the two culprits that typically render them unusable: stains and holes. The good news is that proper washing and storage can usually prevent both.

- **Treat any stains** before you wash your linens. Soaking stained linens in cool water as soon as possible (perhaps right after guests leave) will help prevent any stains from setting, and will allow you to put off machine-washing until the next day. Most durable cotton napkins and tablecloths can be treated with the same stain spray you'd use on your cotton clothes. It's always advisable to test a small portion of a napkin or an inconspicuous corner of a tablecloth first, leaving the rest soaking in cold water in the meantime. Remember that time helps stains to set, as does drying. If you wash your table linens and find that the stains are still there, soak, treat and wash again *before* drying.

Ironing Tips

Table linens only look as good as the job you do ironing them. Here are some tips to help you iron your linens to look their very best.

- Iron clean, damp linens. Spritz them ahead of time and refrigerate overnight for easier ironing, or simply spritz them with water just before ironing.
- Line the ironing board with a terrycloth towel, especially when ironing napkins with a monogram or other embroidery.
- While spray starch is a great tool, use it sparingly and wisely: too much starch makes napkins less soft and even less absorbent, negating some of their best attributes. Most napkin folds require only light starching. If you like lightly scented linens, look for lavender-scented spray starch.
- Linen water, or linen spray, another option for adding subtle scent to ironed table linens (and sheets), is mostly water with a little alcohol and fragrance added. It works well on cotton and linen and comes in such table-friendly scents as ginger, lavender and vanilla. Look for it at Sur La Table (www.surlatable.com) and Bed, Bath, & Beyond (www.bedbathandbeyond.com). Spritz linen water over clean, damp table linens just before ironing.
- Start by ironing linens on the wrong side first, and iron it thoroughly. For darker fabrics, this is the only side you'll be ironing. Press only the wrong side of a monogram or other embroidery.
- Iron with the weave of the cloth and take care not to stretch it as you work. Napkin folds work best with perfectly square napkins, so try to keep them in their original shape.
- For linens that are lighter in color, finish by ironing them briefly on the right side, avoiding any monograms or embroidery.

- **Wash table linens** according to the manufacturer's instructions; most can be machine-washed on a gentle cycle. Gentler soaps are available for vintage linens or any others you want to baby. Cotton napkins can generally be washed the same way you wash your cotton clothes.
- **Store table linens** *only* once they're freshly washed, no matter how unused they look. Not only will stains set when linens are stored soiled, but spots you can't even see have the potential to attract moths and other pests, which can leave holes in your linens. Whether to iron linens before or after storage is a personal choice. I shake out cotton napkins warm from the dryer and loosely fold them for storage, then iron them a day or two before the party. Folded tablecloths can be stored on padded hangers and hung in a closet, or wrapped in acid-free tissue paper and stored in a drawer. Linen napkins should not be stored starched. To avoid dry rot, or fabric rot, store linen napkins flat, if possible; creases (particularly those up the center of the napkin) weaken linen's fibers over time. For the same reason, store linen tablecloths wrapped around a large tube (fabric stores often have extras), rather than folded, if possible.

● **Iron table linens** well ahead of time; it's an integral step to setting a gorgeous table, and it takes time, so don't put it off until the day of the party, when you'll be busy cooking. At least two days before the party, use a spray bottle to liberally spritz your clean linens with water. Roll them up, put them in a plastic bag and refrigerate overnight. When it's time to iron, use spray starch if necessary for extra crispness and set the iron to the setting that suits the fabric type (check the label). For a tablecloth, set up the ironing board near your dining table so you can transfer it gradually to the table as you finish sections.

China and Glassware

Unless you're a bride-to-be planning a postnuptial gathering, you'll probably have to work largely with what you have in terms of china, flatware and glassware. If you *are* a bride-to-be, take this opportunity to register for 12 place settings in each of two china patterns that can be used together: one more neutral and one more decorative. That way, when you have larger dinner parties, you can put the two together for up to 24 place settings.

Even if you have the budget for it (and most of us don't), buying china, flatware and glassware to match each party theme you dream up just wouldn't be practical — that's a lot to store and care for, after all. Fortunately, there are many ways you can perk up your existing place settings for a variety of uses.

Purchase Chargers

Choose silver or gold metallic chargers (consider which one coordinates the best with your existing china) and use them in lieu of placemats, either atop the tablecloth or on a bare table. Silver or gold chargers add instant elegance to your china, they can be used in any season, they're inexpensive (look for them at stores like Target or Zellers) and they take up very little room on the table. I've seen hosts use chargers under everything from multicolored pottery to bone china, and they always elevate the look to special-occasion.

Get Creative with Crafting Supplies

Instead of traditional placemats or chargers, use a colorful 12-inch (30 cm) square sheet of scrapbooking paper (available in craft stores and at Target) underneath each place setting. With the wide variety of colors and designs available, many of them quite elegant, you'll be able to find something that complements your unique theme and color palette. Use the same paper for your invitations.

Buy, Borrow or Rent New Salad or Dessert Plates

If your china is neutral enough, you can successfully pair it with something new. Try sourcing some small plates that can serve as salad or dessert plates in a great new pattern that coordinates with what you already have, and you'll get a whole new look for less. Anthropologie (www.anthropologie.com) often has a selection of interesting and affordable salad and dessert plates that mix and match well. If the china you already have is ornate, choose plates in a solid color to coordinate with it; for a modern look, consider alternative shapes, such as square or oval.

Mix and Match Your Glassware

If you have a great set of crystal wineglasses, then by all means use them. You can dress them up with whimsical wine charms as simple as short lengths of ribbon that coordinate with your party theme and help guests keep track of which glass is theirs. But if you're looking for a change of place setting, consider this: I have a friend who refuses to pay more than $1 for a wineglass, because in her family they break too often. Follow her lead and look for interesting shapes of wineglasses at garage sales, estate sales and thrift stores — if the glass is not part of a large set, so much the better. If each guest has a one-of-a-kind wineglass, it's easy to remember whose is whose, and it's also a lot less upsetting if such a glass breaks: it wasn't expensive, and it wasn't part of a set. For a unified look, stick to clear glasses instead of those with hues.

Silverware

Too many people make the mistake of saving their silverware for special occasions, pulling it out only a couple times a year, if that. If you have it, use it. The more often silver is used, the more attractive it becomes. While new pieces have a blinding shine to them, older pieces develop a patina that shows many years of happy use. The accumulation of small scratches gradually buffs silver to a softer glow. If you're looking forward to developing a perfect patina on your set, be sure to rotate the pieces you use for relatively equal aging. If you've inherited a set from an older relative, it probably already has a nice patina. You can also purchase used silver, either complete sets or mismatched pieces, at estate sales and antique shops. If you question the appeal of a less-than-perfectly-matched set, consider that Napa Style (www.napastyle.com) now offers shoppers that hunted and gathered look by selling mismatched vintage silverware by the pound.

Rental IQ

While renting party supplies costs a lot less than buying them, it can still take a bite out of your budget. If you have to rent tables, chairs, linens, china, flatware and glassware for your party, expect to pay at least $15 per person to do so. But don't take my word on the $15 figure: prices for party rentals vary dramatically depending on your area and needs, so do the research before deciding whether rentals make sense this time around. Look up "party rentals" in the Yellow Pages and get a few quotes. Also keep in mind that the price of oil has affected delivery fees, so be sure to include that cost if you need your rentals delivered. Nearby companies are the best places to start, because they should charge less for delivery than those farther away.

For planning purposes, you should also find out the company's hours of operation (some are closed on Sundays, meaning the goods for a Saturday night party might be parked at your house until Monday morning), contact information (will you be able to reach someone for after-hours emergencies, such as the need to add a tent for inclement weather?) and insurance coverage (who is responsible if there's damage to any of the rentals?).

Here are some ideas for keeping rental costs in check for your party:

- **Forgo delivery, setup and pickup.** Make sure you're clear on what the proposed rental fee includes; all details should be specified in your rental agreement. If the fee includes delivery, setup and pickup, you might be able to shave off some of the price by doing these things yourself — providing you have the right vehicle and a helper.
- **Streamline the details.** Look at the suggested rentals and see where you can cut costs. Maybe you can choose a plainer style of chairs or linens (plain white or cream can make an elegant backdrop that doesn't compete with colorful centerpieces). Maybe you can use a table or two of your own instead of renting all of them. Also, look for any extra items included in the pricing, such as trash bags, that you can purchase for less.
- **Check out the competition.** Once you've trimmed your list down to the basic necessities for your party, get quotes from another rental company or two. You can ask your favorite business if they can match a competitor's price — most will.
- **Know company policies.** Make sure you know the company's payment, reservation and cancellation policies so you don't lose your deposit if you change your mind.

Caring for Your Silverware

If you use your silverware daily, it will tarnish more slowly than if you simply store it. It also helps to store it in a cool place, away from direct sunlight or heat. After using silverware, promptly wash it in hot, soapy water, rinse it and hand-dry it. While most modern silverware is dishwasher-safe (some older types with hollow knife handles are not), put it in an area of the flatware basket away from any stainless steel, to avoid a chemical reaction between the two that can pit silver. Certain foods, such as eggs, salt, broccoli and fish, can cause tarnishing; silverware in contact with these foods will especially benefit from prompt washing.

Even with regular use, silverware will need polishing at least a few times a year. When it's time to polish your set, use a nonabrasive paste. Use a toothbrush if you want to remove tarnish from crevices (some people like to leave tarnish there, as it can accent the design). As an alternative, try my no-rub polishing method: Line a large bowl or plugged kitchen sink with strips of foil. Place the silverware atop the foil and pour in enough boiling water to cover it, then add $\frac{1}{4}$ cup (60 mL) baking soda. Let the silverware soak for 10 minutes, then rinse well and dry with a soft cloth.

Centerpieces

The centerpiece is probably the largest element of decor on your table — and it's the one that most says celebration. We use plates at every meal, but how many of us have a centerpiece on the table for a typical family dinner? Because of its placement and importance, the centerpiece should be given special consideration. It should be highly visible, of course, but not too large: guests should be able to see each other over it at a seated dinner, for instance. The centerpiece is critical in pulling together a party's overall look and theme, so it needs to coordinate with the rest of the decor, including any side arrangements.

Flowers make a traditional and attractive centerpiece (see page 242 for details on flowers). Party favors can also double as centerpieces (for favor ideas, see page 250). Here are some other centerpiece ideas:

- Arrange fruits, vegetables or breads in an attractive basket. This edible display can be eaten in the week following the party, making it both economical and earth-friendly (use any stale bread left over from your display to make French toast, strata or bread pudding). For a lush look, combine a variety of shapes, textures and colors that complement your theme or menu. Depending on the season, consider pomegranates, pears, gourds, pumpkins, melons, heirloom tomatoes, asparagus, lemons, limes, tangerines, coconuts or bananas. Visit specialty or farmers' markets for unusual varieties

that will add more interest to the table. A monochromatic look (all red or all green, for example) can also make a dramatic statement.

- Nothing beats candlelight for flattering lighting — it's no wonder that candles set a romantic, intimate mood for a gathering. Purchase floating candles to place in a bowl filled with water; use that antique candelabrum your grandma left you; set pillar candles of varying heights along a long, narrow tray lined with pressed fall leaves or parchment leaves from a kitchen supply or party store; or create three groupings of candlesticks of varying heights and fit them with long, lean taper candles in a coordinating color.

- Use coffee beans, river rocks or marbles to fill a shallow bowl, square vase or footed candy dish and nestle flower blossoms or tea light candles inside. Coffee beans give off a rich, appetizing aroma; river rocks lend a calm, cool, Zen-like feel to the table; and marbles have a luminescent look and come in a variety of colors to coordinate with any theme.
- Collect organics from the great outdoors. Your backyard might have all you need for an earthy (and free) centerpiece arrangement: cut branches, acorns, nuts, leaves, pine cones. The items can be arranged in bowls or vases, and can be left in their natural state or embellished. A brush of glitter gives earthy elements some holiday sparkle, while spray-painting them silver or gold lends elegance.

Flowers

Fresh flowers, whether cut or potted, add color, fragrance and beauty to your decor and make for an especially attractive centerpiece. Flowers, in fact, are very flexible: they can be selected and arranged to suit themes indoors or out, formal or casual, big-budget or thrifty, whimsical or traditional. In addition to using floral centerpieces, many hosts also use coordinating flower arrangements as accent pieces on side tables, in wall vases or even floating in the backyard pool.

Using flowers as the centerpiece doesn't have to mean sticking to the traditional large single arrangement. In fact, for some themes and some tables, it might make a lot more sense to go for a form that saves space or coordinates better with the party's look. Consider using several small flower arrangements, a garland that winds its way down the center of the table or single blossoms floating in clear bowls.

Flowers can be combined with myriad other elements — fruit, twinkle lights, autumn leaves, greenery — to make a one-of-a-kind centerpiece that suits the season and theme of the party perfectly. You can even mix fresh flowers and silk flowers together (as in the photograph at right). Since silk flowers can be reused, this idea could cut your costs significantly over the course of years of dinner parties!

Pretty potted flowering plants, such as hyacinths, azaleas and chrysanthemums, make an attractive alternative to cut flowers. The advantages are that you can purchase them up to a week ahead, use them on your table for the party and then replant them in your yard after the event. For the party, place potted plants in an attractive container (a simple terracotta pot or a pretty piece of pottery) that's slightly larger than the plastic pot they came in.

Using a Florist

If you don't trust yourself with flower arranging (or sense that you already have your hands full with other party tasks) but *do* want a floral centerpiece or multiple arrangements, there are plenty of professionals who'd be happy to step in. If you decide to work with a florist, it makes sense to select someone whose sense of

Flower Seasonality Chart

Name of Flower	Colors
Spring	
Anemone	White, pink, red, purple
Baby's breath	White
Bachelor's button	White, pink, red, blue
Bells of Ireland	Green
Boronia	Pink
Calla lily	White, yellow
Calla lily, mini	Most colors
Carnations	Most colors
Casablanca lily	White
Daffodil	Yellow
Delphinium	White, blue
Gardenia	White
Gladiolus	Many colors
Heather	Pink, lavender
Hyacinth	White, pink, purple
Lilac	White, violet
Lily of the valley	White, pink
Narcissus	White
Orchid	Most colors
Peony	White, pink, red
Protea	Pink
Ranunculus	White, pink, orange, red, yellow
Rose	Most colors
Scabiosa	White, pink, purple
Stargazer lily	White, pink
Sweetpea	White, pink, red, peach, purple
Tulip	Most colors
Waxflower	White, pink
Summer	
Alstromeria	White, pink, yellow, orange
Aster	White, pink, purple
Baby's breath	White

Name of Flower	Colors
Summer	
Bachelor's button	White, pink, red, blue
Bells of Ireland	Green
Calla lily	White, yellow
Calla lily, mini	Most colors
Carnations	Most colors
Chrysanthemum	White, pink, yellow, orange
Cockscomb	Pink, yellow, red, green
Columbine	White, pink, yellow, orange, red, purple
Delphinium	White, purple, blue
Lavender	Purple
Forget-me-not	Blue, pink, white
Freesia	White, pink, yellow, blue, purple
Gardenia	White
Gladiolus	Many colors
Gerbera daisy	White, pink, yellow, orange, red
Heather	Pink, lavender
Hydrangea	White, pink, purple, blue
Iris	White, purple, blue
Larkspur	White, pink, purple, blue
Liatris	Pink, purple
Lily	White, pink, yellow, orange
Lily of the valley	White, pink
Lisianthus	White, pink, purple
Orchid	Most colors
Protea	Pink
Queen Anne's lace	White
Rose	Most colors
Scabiosa	White, pink, purple
Snapdragons	White, pink, yellow, orange

Name of Flower	Colors
Summer	
Solidaster	Yellow
Statice	Purple, white
Stephanotis	White
Sunflower	Yellow, orange
Tuberose	White
Yarrow	White, pink, yellow, red
Zinnia	Pink, red, orange
Fall	
Aster	White, pink, purple
Baby's breath	White
Bachelor's button	White, pink, red, blue
Cabbage, ornamental	White, pink, purple, green
Calla lily	White, yellow
Calla lily, mini	Most colors
Carnations	Most colors
Chrysanthemum	White, pink, yellow, orange
Dahlia	Most colors
Delphinium	White, purple, blue
Gardenia	White
Gladiolus	Many colors
Heather	Pink, lavendar
Lily of the valley	White, pink
Orchid	Most colors
Protea	Pink
Marigold	Yellow, red, orange
Rose	Most colors
Scabiosa	White, pink, purple
Statice	Purple, white
Zinnia	Pink, red, orange
Winter	
Amaryllis	White, pink, red
Anemone	White, pink, red, blue
Baby's breath	White

Name of Flower	Colors
Winter	
Bachelor's button	White, pink, red, blue
Bells of Ireland	Green
Calla lily	White, yellow
Calla lily, mini	Most colors
Camellia	White, pink
Carnations	Most colors
Casablanca lily	White
Cosmos	White, pink, yellow, orange
Daffodil	Yellow
Delphinium	White, purple, blue
Dogwood	White, yellow
Forget-me-not	Blue, pink, white
Gardenia	White
Gladiolus	Many colors
Heather	Pink, lavender
Holly	Green, red berries
Jasmine	White
Lily of the valley	White, pink
Narcissus	White, yellow
Nurine lily	White, pink, purple
Orchid	Most colors
Poinsettia	White, pink, red
Protea	Pink
Ranunculus	White, pink, red, orange, yellow
Rose	Most colors
Scabiosa	White, pink, purple
Stargazer lily	White, pink
Star of Bethlehem	White
Sweetpea	White, pink, red, purple
Tulip	Most colors
Waxflower	White, pink

style meshes well with your own and who seems open to applying his or her expertise to the unique occasion you have in mind, for custom (rather than prefabricated) results. Be upfront and detailed about your ideas, naming specific flowers you have in mind and sharing pictures of arrangements you especially like. Use the flower seasonality guide (page 244) as a starting point, so that your choices will be in season — meaning they should be abundantly available and also (hopefully) less expensive.

Do-It-Yourself Flower Arranging

If you don't mind taking the time and summoning the creativity to design and put together your own floral arrangements, you'll save a bit of money and will have complete control over the outcome. Here are some tips for do-it-yourself flower arranging:

- Plan to arrange the flowers the day before the party and store them in a cool place overnight to keep them at their freshest.
- Incorporate flowers, herbs, leaves and other organic elements you have growing on your property — or visit a farmers' market for locally grown, freshly cut flowers.
- Remove any foliage that will be underwater and cut stems on an angle, trimming at least 1 inch (2.5 cm) from the bottom of the stem. To avoid crushing the stems, cut flowers one at a time, placing each stem in water immediately after cutting it.
- Use warm water and add fresh-cut flower food (from the florist) or a little bit of sugar to keep flowers fresher for longer.
- Place chicken wire across the mouth of the vase to hold stems in place. Conceal it with part of the arrangement or with decorative ribbon.
- Keep it low: short arrangements are easier to make than tall ones — and for seated dinners, they're also easier to see over, which makes for better conversation.
- If you're a beginner, go for a monochromatic look, choosing a single type of flower in one color, such as white roses or purple irises. Even inexpensive carnations are impressive when several are bunched together into a tightly bound puff.
- For an airy, open look, gently peel back the petals of tulips or roses (or try blowing on them to encourage them to open on their own).
- If you have only a few flowers to work with, use a clear vase or container with a narrow neck and a wide base, or fill a wider-mouthed glass vase with pebbles, marbles or fruit (cranberries or wedges of lemons or lime, for example) to help keep the flowers in place *and* add color and texture to the look.

Seating Plans

When you're entertaining six or more for a seated dinner, you'll want to give some thought to where people will sit, planning it out ahead of time and using place cards to realize that vision. Smart seating can promote good conversation and split up strong personalities, delicately balancing the chemistry of a party so that it's as interesting as it can be without veering into territory that's too intense. Smart seating can also make the party feel more inclusive for those who are shy or newer to the group.

The classic etiquette books say that the host and hostess should occupy the heads of the table, at opposite ends; a male guest of honor should be seated at the hostess's right and a female guest of honor at the host's right; couples should be seated separately; and all guests should be seated to alternate between male and female, when possible. All that protocol is really just a tried-and-true method for encouraging conversation among people who might not know each other as well, and discouraging best friends or longtime couples from intense conversations with one another rather than getting to know their newer dining companions. Couples who protest being seated apart can be reassured that with this plan, they will have much more to talk about at the end of the night.

Potential problem pairings should be seated far away from one another (your radical right-wing neighbor and your lefty activist friend, for instance), and anyone especially shy should be placed near a great conversationalist who can help engage them in the conversation. Use your place cards to help bring out the best in each of your guests, and your guests will bring out the best in your party.

Place Cards

Given the importance of place cards to a seated dinner party's dynamic, it's a good idea to include them in your tabletop decor for any dinner party of six or more. You'll find commercially printed place cards at any store that has a good selection of stationery, from office supply chains to fine stationers to arts and crafts stores. Search the Internet and you'll find place card templates that can be downloaded and printed. Creative hosts and hostesses can make their own place cards by hand, with card stock and an elegant pen — and perhaps pretty edges made with pinking shears or creative touches that pick up on the party's theme. Craft stores have an inspiring collection of supplies; the scrapbooking aisle offers all the necessary embellishments, punches and other tools.

When it's time to write names in, you'll need to decide how to word them. First names only? First and last names? What about courtesy titles? Let the formality and size of the event guide you, as well as how well your guests are likely to know each other. I like the personal look of handwritten place cards, with first names for smaller groups and first and last names for larger groups. Computer-printed place cards are a good option for those with poor handwriting, but they do tend to feel more corporate.

While many retailers sell place card holders that keep everyone's names upright, they're not always necessary. Several of the napkin folds in this book have a pocket or fold that works well as a place card holder. And many commercially produced place cards are made

Invitations

Creating and sending out invitations is the first step when you're planning your party, so it's smart to start early. Send out invitations at least two weeks in advance for most at-home parties, up to a month in advance around the holidays and at other especially busy times, and at least six weeks in advance for a formal occasion, such as a wedding. (For weddings and other events that include out-of-towners, send save-the-dates up to a year in advance, to allow guests to make travel plans.)

There are many ways to extend an invitation. While nobody can deny the charm of receiving a paper invitation in the mail, it's also fine to send a simple email, to create an event on a social networking site, to use virtual invitations like those at Evite (www.evite.com) or even to make the invitation by phone.

Your invitations should contain all the important details that let guests know what to expect: how to dress, what to bring, where to go and when to be there. Here's a quick rundown of what should be on your invitations (or included in your verbal invitation).

- **Who.** Guests need to know who's hosting the party and how to contact them (by phone, email or text). It can also be helpful to briefly mention who's invited — "work friends," "neighborhood friends" or "family," for example; an indication such as "adults only" or "kids welcome" makes your preferences clear.
- **What and why.** Explain the party's theme and the reason you're throwing it, whether for a guest of honor or a special occasion. This will help guests decide how to dress and what, if anything, they'd like to bring.
- **When.** It's a no-brainer that your guests need to know the date and starting time of the party. Smart dinner party hosts plan a cocktail hour (or 45 minutes) at the beginning of their party to ensure that everyone will be there when it's time to sit down at the table. With some crowds, it's helpful to include an ending time as well, as is the practice for open houses and children's birthday parties.
- **Where.** Guests need the address of the party at the very least; a map is a helpful extra. If parking is a problem in your neighborhood, it's nice to let guests know about that free lot around the corner. When you're hosting a party away from home, you'll want to include the address and phone number of the destination, and perhaps its website address, as well as parking information. If you've arranged for valet parking, make sure to say so.
- **How.** Let invitees know how you'll be celebrating, whether it's just eating and drinking or the plans include playing games or dancing. Informed guests will arrive ready to participate — and wearing the right shoes, too.

with a notecard-like fold-over design that stands up quite well on its own. Some crafty hosts enclose each place card in a small frame for a picture-perfect presentation, or let a small framed photo of each guest stand in for his or her name, making a fun take-home favor.

Party Favors

Since the Renaissance, marrying couples of means (and generosity) have been giving their guests party favors, but any third-grader can tell you that party favors are always welcome at a party, from kids' birthdays to grownup dinners. Some fancy restaurants even send their guests home with a jar of house-made jam, a printed menu from the evening or a box of candies from the chef. The point? Such small gifts let guests know that their presence was anticipated and appreciated, and they also serve as a memento of the occasion — it makes the fun last just a little longer. Party favors aren't a requirement, but who doesn't love a present?

Party favors become part of the decor, so it's important to match them to the overall theme of your event. Especially attractive favors can even do double duty as your centerpiece. While looks are important, it's also thoughtful to choose something your guests can actually use. (It's anyone's guess how many children's birthday party "goody bags" wind up in the trash.) Consider gifts that can be used up, such as candles or candies, or gifts that your guests will continue to enjoy, such as potted herbs or recipes.

RSVPs

Basic etiquette, even in the modern world, requires that you respond to an invitation, particularly one that clearly states "RSVP," the French way of saying "Please respond." But as frustrated party hosts everywhere can attest, more often than not, you might as well be asking in Greek.

I've catered more than 10,000 parties over the last few decades, and my take on RSVPs is: ask, but don't expect to receive. Typically, you can count on half of your invitees showing up. But while that formula works well for a cocktail party or potluck, it's not adequate for seated dinner parties, when you need to know exactly how many places to set. Feel free to call, email or text any stragglers a couple of days before the event so you can finalize your headcount as well as your shopping list. When dealing with sensitive types, I often pretend I'm checking to make sure that they received the invitation and that they don't have any food allergies or other dietary restrictions.

You'll improve your chances of hearing back if you put an email address and a cellphone number prominently on the invitation, as well as a deadline for responding. While people seem to put off making actual person-to-person phone calls these days, they're often more responsive by text or email, which can be sent any time of day or night and read when it's convenient.

The easiest way to present favors is to arrange them at each place setting, but if your party doesn't involve place settings, you can set a large basket of parting gifts, with name tags on them, in a visible location near the door and enlist the help of a friend to make sure departing friends know to take one. For larger parties, ask a friend to serve as "exit hostess" to pass out favors as guests leave or, if you intend to have valet service, ask the valet to hand them out as guests get into their cars.

Choose from any of the following ideas, or use them as inspiration for creating your own unique party favors.

10 Fun Favors

Make the party favors festive, and they'll serve as a take-home reminder for your guests of the fantastic time they had at your shindig. Here are 10 of my favorite fun favors to send home with guests.

1. **Hot cocoa mix.** Pack a small clear glass jar, such as a Mason jar, with hot cocoa mix (use an online recipe to make your own with cocoa powder, sugar and powdered milk, or buy prepared

hot cocoa mix in bulk and divide it among jars). Mix in some mini marshmallows, if you like, or add them to the top; they work perfectly as filler. Tie a seasonal ribbon around the top of the jar and attach preparation instructions. When the weather's warm, you can prepare the mix for "frozen hot chocolate," with instructions to blend it with milk and ice.

2. **Beef jerky.** Do you take pride in the high-quality meat you serve your guests? Send some home with them by making homemade beef jerky; the drying process makes it shelf-stable, and it will make for a satisfying snack for later on. If you think your guests might own a food dehydrator and have the motivation to try making jerky themselves, you can also provide a recipe card revealing your methods. Visit the USDA website at www.fsis.usda.gov for food safety guidelines regarding homemade jerky.

3. **Fortune cookies.** Make homemade fortune cookies containing your own original fortunes. Whether they take it home as a favor or open it just after dinner, your guests will be amazed when their message is more personal and on the mark than the typical one. While fortune cookie recipes are available online, many people have success using a tuile recipe. (French tuiles are traditionally almond-flavored; they're thin, crisp cookies that can be molded into shape while hot.) If your guests include avid bakers, print out the recipe you used for each to take home, too.

4. **Snack mix.** Do you make a fantastic party snack mix that your guests can't seem to get enough of? Send some home with them as a favor you know they'll enjoy. Make twice as much snack mix as you'll need for the party and pack small clear bags with a take-home portion for each guest, tied with a seasonal ribbon. You'll find clear treat bags at baking supply stores and craft stores like Michaels (www.michaels.com). Print out the recipe on card stock, punch a hole in one corner and attach it to the ribbon so they can make it themselves. This idea works well with anything from old-school Chex mix (recipes for both savory and sweet versions are available at www.chex.com) to candied or spiced mixed nuts to your own special blend of trail mix.

5. **Mixed CDs.** Are you hosting a Hawaiian Luau (page 318) with mellow island tunes? A Wine and Cheese Tasting (page 296) featuring songs from Italian or French artists? If you've gone to the trouble of creating a themed playlist for your party, you've already done most of the work necessary to create a great favor. Simply burn mixed CDs of the playlist — or at least 10 to 15 songs from it — so your guests will get to keep enjoying it after the party's over. Even if the music isn't as obviously connected to the party's theme, a party playlist always makes a fun favor. You'll only need to make one CD per couple.

6. **Pampering products.** What better favor could there be for the Girls' Night In party (page 300) or any ladies-only gathering? Every woman likes to try new products. Assemble small bags or baskets of travel-size pampering products, such as bubble bath, bath oils, body wash, body lotions, scrubs or masks. Most drugstores carry inexpensive travel-size bottles, while more indulgent products (and prettier packaging) can be found at stores such as Bath and Body Works (www.bathandbodyworks. com), L'Occitane (www.usa.loccitane.com) and Aveda (www. aveda.com). Another fun source for all things travel-sized is Minimus (www.minimus.biz).

7. **Oil and vinegar.** This amazing duo can join forces to create salad dressings, marinades or a divine bread dip, making it a great favor for friends who love to cook (and eat). Purchase a small bottle of each for every guest or couple, or look for an already packaged decorative combination, such as those sold at World Market (www.worldmarket.com). For small parties, a decorative glass oil and vinegar cruet can be fun — one per couple, of course. Those who don't have a cruet at their place can be given a whisk instead, for mixing the oil and vinegar.

8. **Travel games.** If you're hosting a Friends' Game Night (page 302), sending your guests home with a new game can help extend the spirit of the party. Look for travel-sized games that will help make their next trip more fun. Hasbro makes travel versions of many of its popular games, including Battleship, Sorry and

Connect Four. Books of crossword puzzles or Sudoku, which are available in levels from kid-friendly to genius, and game paraphernalia such as a new set of dice or a deck of playing cards also make great favors. Check out American Science & Surplus (www.sciplus.com) for interesting and inexpensive games.

9. **Gardening kit.** For any outdoor brunch or lunch, such as the Garden Brunch party (page 274), a small gardening kit makes a fitting take-home favor. You can find windowsill herb garden kits, prepackaged with small pots, peat and seeds, at home goods stores. An inexpensive alternative is a package of seeds that are easy to grow and ready to sow the season you give them — try mixed baby lettuces, basil or cherry tomatoes. Choose one larger packet of organic seeds that has a pretty label, such as those from Botanical Interests (www.botanicalinterests.com), or pair up two (or more) small packets of seeds and tie them together with a pretty ribbon.

10. **Mini bottle of bubbly.** Celebrating something? It doesn't get more festive than Champagne or sparkling wine. Many winemakers (as fancy as Moet et Chandon and as affordable as Korbel) now offer one-quarter-size bottles of bubbly, sometimes sold in four-packs — or even by the case online. A mini bottle makes a fun favor and can double as a place card holder for a seated dinner: attach each guest's name with a ribbon and set the bottle above or even atop the dinner plate. Champagne makes a fun favor for a New Year's Eve party, an anniversary dinner, a big birthday celebration or any other time you have cause to clink glasses.

10 Sentimental Favors

Are you planning a special couple's Valentine's Day dinner? A going-away party for a favorite neighbor or friend? A bridal shower? A graduation party for your (gulp!) baby? Here are fitting favors when the occasion calls for sweet, sentimental or romantic gestures that show your guests how much you care.

1. **Custom T-shirts.** When you want to remember a significant day, such as a graduation or milestone birthday, give yourself and each of your guests a wearable memento of the important occasion you spent together. Purchase white T-shirts, buying enough that each guest and host has one, plus a few spares just in case. Go one size larger for each guest than you think you need, and look for multi-packs to save money. Cover a table with newspaper or plastic to protect it, and set up containers of permanent fabric markers so your guests can decorate their own shirts, as well as signing each other's. Place cardboard inside the shirts to prevent bleed-through.

2. **Custom frames.** Provide an inexpensive frame for each guest to decorate according to the occasion. Faux jewels and acrylic paints will be fun for adults and older kids, while foam stickers and pom-poms are perfect for preschoolers. Provide a photograph for each finished frame, either of the group or of the guest of honor, or take photos at the party and mail one to each guest for his or her frame the next week. Alternatively, you can have children craft the frame, adding a photograph of themselves before giving it to a parent or grandparent.

3. **Massage goodies.** For a couples-only Valentine's Day party, encourage your guests to indulge each other (once they get home, of course) by providing each with a bottle of massage oil in such relaxing scents as vanilla, lavender or rosemary. You could alternate oils with old-fashioned wooden rolling massagers for every other guest, so couples get one of each.

4. **Homemade sweets.** Do you make a mean batch of brownies? Delectable chocolate truffles? Incomparable sugar cookies?

Elevate your best confections with pretty packaging, making them into attractive favors. Visit a crafts or baking supply store for small heart-shaped boxes, candy boxes or clear treat bags. As an alternative, you can make heart-shaped sugar cookies and frost them with each guest's name as edible place cards that can be taken home or eaten at the party. For a children's party, set out unembellished sugar cookies with frostings and sprinkles and let them decorate their own.

5. **Scented candles.** A pretty scented candle in a tin canister makes a welcome gift for almost any guest. While the tin makes it a travel-worthy candle that can warm up a hotel room, it can just as easily be enjoyed at home. When it makes sense to do so, choose scents that evoke your party's theme. You'll find candles in holiday aromas, such as gingerbread, and in fresh herbal or exotic fruit scents.

6. **Love songs.** For a romantic dinner party, make your own custom mix of love songs both to play at the party and to burn onto CDs as favors for your friends. It's fun to mix old-fashioned songs with more contemporary ones, giving the collection something that speaks to everyone and increasing the chance that you'll introduce friends to something new.

7. **Valentine candy.** For a kids' Valentine's Day party, fill flat-bottomed ice cream cones with red, white and pink M&Ms, presenting them on a tray at the end of the party so children can take one on their way home. Mini muffin cups or bonbon cups also make creative holders for Valentine candies.

8. **Cool ice.** Look for heart-shaped ice cube trays at local crafts stores or home goods stores, and set one at each guest's place. (Don't forget fun ice for other themes, too: you can find trays for making many different shapes, including dinosaurs and jewels.)

9. **Hand towels.** Pretty seasonal guest towels or personalized master bath hand towels are a nice touch that your friends will enjoy having in their home. If you want to go all out, consider having his-and-hers monogrammed hand towels made; if you want to keep it dialed down, choose paper guest towels rubber-stamped with the initial of each guest's last name, or in a design that fits the season or theme of your party. Consider personalizing hand towels with embroidery or, even easier, embroidered appliqués (check local fabric stores).

10. **Baking kit.** Assemble a baking kit that includes a high-quality sugar cookie mix you like. For Valentine's Day, pair it with a heart-shaped cookie cutter. For other occasions, look for a corresponding cookie cutter: diplomas or graduation caps, wedding cakes or bride-and-groom designs, baby motifs — there are endless choices available. Attach a recipe for frosting, if you like.

10 Kids' Favors

Few guests appreciate a party favor as much as your youngest invitees. Charm them with one of these favors, and remember that it's okay to let them open and play with your gift early on. For young children, favors do double duty, keeping them busy — and therefore sitting nicely at the table or playing quietly — a little longer than they otherwise would. You can consider it a favor for their parents, too.

1. **Outdoor games.** Sometimes simplest is best: a package of sidewalk chalk, a container of bubbles, a balsa wood airplane, a kaleidoscope or a butterfly net — even from the local dollar store — can keep young children happily occupied and enjoying the great outdoors.

2. **Explorer tools.** Set up a scavenger hunt for young guests in your backyard, outfitting them with toy compasses, binoculars and magnifying glasses to aid them in their explorations. Small screened-in bug-catchers to house their finds can also be fascinating for some kids. Check out American Science & Surplus (www.sciplus.com) for inexpensive toys and projects with a scientific bent.

3. **Bag of tricks.** Provide little hams with a gift bag of three or so friendly gags that will help them elicit laughs, if mostly from themselves and each other. Whoopee cushions, googly-eye glasses, fake teeth, disappearing ink, snake-in-a-can, hand buzzers and the old bug-in-an-ice cube trick will have a whole new generation giggling. Check out Partypalooza for great gags (www.partypalooza.com).

4. **Painting set.** For big kids, a small paint-by-numbers set in a theme that interests them can be a satisfying artistic endeavor for during or after the party, with results they'll be proud to hang up at home. Younger children will love a fresh set of washable watercolor paints and a pad of thick paper to go with it. A good online source for paint-by-number sets for all skill levels is Oak Ridge Hobbies (www.oakridgehobbies.com).

5. **Drawing set.** For young children, purchase a small coloring book in a theme that suits their age and interests, and present it with a fresh set of crayons; let them color at the table during dinner, if they like. Older kids will enjoy a sketchpad and a set of colored pencils.

6. **Modeling clay.** While Play-Doh isn't technically clay — it's a "modeling compound" — kids don't care; they'll amuse themselves shaping it, smashing it and reshaping it all over again. For longer playing at the table, provide vinyl placemats and small rolling pins and cookie cutters to assist them in their designs. Crafty teenagers might enjoy working with Fimo,

a polymer clay that can be formed into beads and pendants (among other decorative items) and then baked in the oven to harden. Vibrant Fimo beads make for one-of-a-kind necklaces. Great ideas can be found on Fimo's website: www.fimo.com.

7. **Activity books.** Activity books run the gamut from preschool connect-the-dots pictures to challenging Sudoku puzzles. Classic Mad Libs are always good for a laugh, and old-fashioned crossword puzzles or word searches can challenge big kids. Be sure to provide a pencil for each guest.

8. **Baking mix in a jar.** A homemade chocolate chip cookie mix or brownie mix layered in a large Mason jar or clear acrylic jar (look for instructions online) makes a fun take-home for big kids who like to get involved in the kitchen. For younger kids, pack the mix in a bag (so it won't break if dropped). Either way, add a tag with mixing and baking instructions.

9. **Chocolate factory.** Pack gift bags with a package of chocolate disks, a small chocolate mold and instructions so kids can, with their parents' help, make their own chocolate candy. Your local arts and crafts or cake supply store will have all of the materials you need. Molds come in many designs to suit the season or occasion.

10. **Gift tower.** Buy three sizes of small trinket boxes (see photos, page 248) and fill each with various treats for your young guests to open, stacking them largest to smallest atop each child's plate. Choose a larger item for the largest box; depending on the theme, you could stuff it with an accessory they can wear at the party, a pre-dinner snack or a small game. Tuck colorful candies into the medium box and put a small object, such as a balloon, in the smallest box.

10 Holiday Favors

Winter holidays are an entertaining season unto themselves, deserving of their own set of party favor ideas. If you're hosting a party (or even if you just need a hostess gift suitable for the holidays), scan this list for favor ideas that fit the occasion.

1. **Tea towels.** Whether you think of them as tea towels or dish towels, a holiday version of this everyday item can make anyone's kitchen more festive. Look for the kind preprinted with a sugar cookie recipe, buy one with a cookie cutter attached or roll up a set of two or three holiday tea towels and attach a card with a pretty ribbon.

2. **Holiday gift.** While you have all your friends over, why not give them their holiday gift as a favor, so you can enjoy watching them open it? An inexpensive beaded necklace, bracelet or set of earrings presented in a see-through organza bag is wonderful for the ladies (see photo, page 294). For men, try a holiday CD or a bottle of wine.

3. **Candy.** Truffles, toffee, rum balls —what kind of candy you choose almost matters less than how it's presented. Look for small gold or silver treat boxes and fill them with one or two decadent candies for each guest (see photo, page 294).

4. **Rosemary tree.** Small rosemary plants cut into the shape of Christmas trees are often available at local nurseries and upscale markets at this time of year. If you're entertaining a group of ladies, get one for each; when couples come over, give them one to share. These fragrant topiaries smell wonderful, can be used as needed for cooking and can even be planted outside later on.

5. **Gingerbread or pumpkin bread loaves.** These breads come together quickly, smell wonderful while baking, are easy to wrap up for a pretty presentation and freeze well. With the abundance of cookies given at this time of year, a breakfast treat is always a welcome break. Look for mini loaf pans that hold four or eight loaves apiece.

6. **Taper candles.** People go through a lot of taper candles during the holidays; if it's not an Advent wreath or a menorah, it's simply the candlesticks on the dining room table or sideboard. Tie pretty taper candles together with a holiday ribbon and set at each place for a practical, yet elegant favor.

7. **Coffee or tea.** An aromatic bag of coffee or a stash of tea leaves goes perfectly with all the sweet treats we eat around the holidays — and it will keep until the New Year without any fuss. Pickier palates will appreciate whole-bean coffee or loose-leaf tea; others love the convenience of Starbucks' VIA Ready Brew instant coffee packets or high-quality teabags for the office or busy days at home.

8. **Holiday DVD or Blu-ray.** A DVD or Blu-ray of a favorite holiday flick gives your guests a great excuse to sit down at home and take a break from the hubbub for a couple of hours. Choose a cozy favorite you think your friends will enjoy, and buy one for each individual or couple. For the other half of each couple, you could put together a bag of microwave popcorn and hot cocoa to enjoy with the movie.

9. **Holiday ornament.** Those who decorate a Christmas tree every year often enjoy remembering the story behind each ornament as they hang it. Become part of your friends' collective history by purchasing a Christmas ornament for each invitee. Use a metallic paint pen to write the year and perhaps the occasion on each ornament. They'll bring extra holiday sparkle to your table setting, too.

10. **Wine.** How about a bottle of bubbly for New Year's? You can either spring for full-size bottles or purchase a cute split for each person at the party. Attach a card with your holiday and New Year's wishes, or use a paint pen to write your message directly on each bottle. A red or white wine that would go well with a holiday meal is another good choice.

Etiquette for the 21st Century

Party guests, want to be invited back? Party hosts, want to impress? Here are some 21st-century etiquette tips for those on both sides of the table.

If you're a guest:
- When you receive an invitation, RSVP promptly and ask what you can bring. When your host says you don't need to bring anything, plan to bring something anyway — but nothing that requires care the night of the party (see suggestions on page 266).
- Show up reasonably on time, within 15 to 25 minutes after the party begins. Never, ever arrive early "to help" unless you've specifically been asked to do so.
- If you are running more than 30 minutes late for a seated dinner, call and let your host know when you will arrive so he or she can make an informed decision about whether to hold dinner.
- Turn off your cellphone when you get to the party. If you must be reachable, as on-call emergency personnel — or as a parent — put your phone on vibrate; if you must answer it, do so away from the table.
- Engage other guests in interesting but non-threatening conversation; avoid divisive political or religious issues. Make an effort to include guests who are shy or seem otherwise left out.
- If you have strict dietary restrictions, let your host know when you RSVP, offering to bring a dish that suits your diet while complementing the meal that is planned — and prepare enough to share. Avoid commenting on what is or is not on other people's plates.
- Offer to help clear the table or serve as needed. If your help is declined, keep your seat and contribute to the conversation.
- Leave on time. The meal is finished, you've enjoyed an after-dinner drink, and your hosts are beginning to yawn? Time to call it a night.
- Send your thanks the next day. A quick call, email or text will do, but a mailed thank-you card is never forgotten.
- Return the invitation by asking your hosts over within the next few months, if possible.

If you're the host:
- Issue a written or verbal invitation at least two weeks in advance, providing all pertinent details so nobody shows up dressed for the wrong occasion or feels silly for not bringing a birthday present (to an event they didn't realize was a birthday party).
- Let guests know, in general terms, who else is invited ("work friends" or "neighbors"), especially if it's a small group.

- Accept help from close friends who would like to bring a dish. Collaborative efforts are often more fun for everyone involved. Some hosts like to maintain tight control of the menu, assigning dishes, while others feel more open to on-the-fly contributions. If you're the former type, keep your assignments to close friends who insist on bringing something, and give them a couple of choices, if possible. (Not everyone wants to make tiramisu for 20.)
- Prepare the meal ahead of time so you can enjoy visiting with your guests. If it gets close to party time and you're not ready, abandon a dish or take a shortcut (baked potatoes instead of potato gratin) rather than remaining stressed out and unavailable after your guests arrive.
- Make brief introductions among people who don't know each other, pointing out any similar interests so they can pick up the conversation easily.
- Keep the mood light by remaining cheerful in the face of red wine spills or latecomers; if you appear to take the hiccups in stride, your guests will feel more comfortable.
- Unless your guests are family members or overnight guests, leave the dishes for later and enjoy spending time with your visitors.

Host or Hostess Gifts

When you're on the receiving end of a party invitation, you'll want to bring a small token to show your appreciation. It's considerate to choose a gift that won't require any immediate attention from your busy host or hostess — who wants to risk burning the crostini while they find a vase for those flowers? Here are some favorite host or hostess gifts that are always appreciated.

- **Wine.** Wine is almost always welcome. Let the party-giver decide whether to open it the night of the party or save it for another time.
- **Liquor.** For party hosts who favor mixed drinks, consider a bottle of vodka, gin or rum; they might also enjoy flavored rim sugar and festive paper cocktail napkins.
- **Plants.** Choose a house or patio plant instead of cut flowers. Potted herbs such as basil, rosemary or mint are fragrant and practical in warmer months. In winter, look for an amaryllis or paperwhite bulb kit.
- **Chocolate.** Choose truffles, an assortment of high-quality chocolate bars or a generous chunk of Valrhona or Callebaut dark chocolate for a baking enthusiast.
- **Cheese.** A round of Brie, a brick of sharp white Cheddar or an ample wedge of blue cheese can be enjoyed now or later on.
- **Music.** Choose a CD that can be used for entertaining, with a gift receipt attached if you're unsure of what they have in their collection.
- **Tea towels.** Pretty printed tea towels are a versatile gift, useful for drying dishes, lining bread baskets or standing in as hand towels in the guest bathroom.
- **Candles.** Look for elegant taper candles for the table or a botanical-scented kitchen candle in a jar or tin.
- **Breakfast treats.** Who wouldn't love to wake up the morning after throwing a party to a pastry box full of croissants or a pan of cinnamon rolls? Include instructions for reheating.
- **Coffee or tea.** Coffee lovers will appreciate a bag of whole-bean coffee; tea aficionados will adore a stash of loose-leaf tea, perhaps paired with a scone baking mix.
- **Stationery.** Purchase pretty notecards, blank on the inside, that can be used for any occasion.
- **Soaps.** Look for elegant guest soaps monogrammed with the first letter of your host's last name.

Pulling the Look Together

You've chosen your linens, china, tabletop accessories, centerpiece and flowers. Now it's time to pull the look together. Set the table or set up the buffet at least one day before the party, complete with linens, china, flatware and glassware. Place a sticky note on each serving plate to indicate what food goes where. If your centerpiece is not floral, you can place it on the table now too; if it is, you'll want to keep it cool until the day of the party. If you have a cat that's likely to walk on the table, hold off on the wineglasses and cover the rest of it with a clean bed sheet until party time.

Setting up a day ahead will prevent you from forgetting anything crucial that could add to last-minute mayhem, such as ironing table linens, polishing tarnished silver or rinsing out dusty wineglasses. During your last-minute preparations, you'll thank yourself for having a pristine table ready and waiting for the food, whether you're hosting a sit-down dinner or a more casual buffet meal.

Setting the Table for a Sit-Down Meal

For the typical family-style meal, each place usually needs just one plate, one water glass, perhaps a wineglass, a napkin and basic flatware — a fork, a knife and possibly a spoon. But when company's coming, or when the occasion calls for a more formal meal, a parade of flatware, glassware and china ensues and many people start to feel a lot less certain about what goes where.

Here are some general rules of thumb for the person setting the table (as well as the person seated at the table). Flatware is used from the outside in. For instance, if the first course is a salad, you'll place the salad fork to the outside, or left, of the dinner fork. If the first course is a soup, place the soup spoon to the outside, or right, of the knife. Dessert forks and spoons are placed horizontally above each place setting, where they'll be out of the way during dinner. Alternatively, they can be brought out after the dinner dishes are cleared.

For china, the first course plate or bowl is placed atop the dinner plate, and the bread and butter plate is set to the upper left of the dinner plate. For glassware, a water glass is set to the upper right of the dinner plate, with a wineglass to the lower right of the water glass. When more than one type of wine will be served, place the glass for the first wine closest to the water glass, and the wineglass for each subsequent course to the lower right of the previous glass.

Formal Dinner Setting

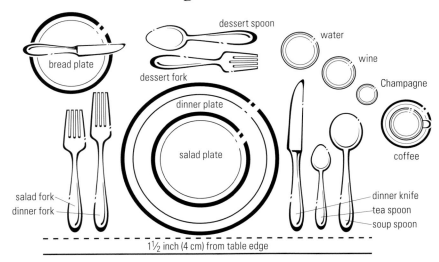

dessert spoon

water

wine

Champagne

bread plate

dessert fork

dinner plate

coffee

salad plate

salad fork

dinner fork

dinner knife

tea spoon

soup spoon

1½ inch (4 cm) from table edge

Casual Dinner Setting

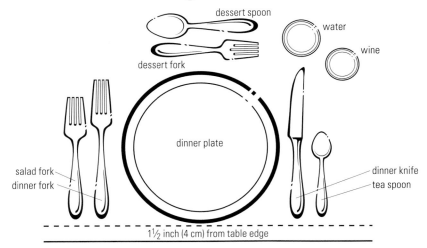

dessert spoon

water

wine

dessert fork

dinner plate

salad fork

dinner fork

dinner knife

tea spoon

1½ inch (4 cm) from table edge

Setting a Beautiful Buffet

Is there any more sensible way to serve a large crowd than by setting up a buffet? With this arrangement, the food is gorgeously presented all at once and guests help themselves, making it a lot easier on a host or hostess who doesn't have the benefit of a staff. Buffets also encourage mixing and mingling; with no set places, guests are free to enjoy their meal wherever they like. (A table and chairs can also be set up away from the buffet table for guests who aren't comfortable balancing a plate and wineglass on their laps.)

Buffets are also ideal setups for entertaining when you're short on space in your dining room. A single 6- to 8-foot (180 to 240 cm) dining-room table can hold enough food, plates, flatware and napkins for as many as 50 guests. But pulling off such a party takes thoughtful arranging. On page 270, you'll find some tips on setting up the best buffet. For more help, see the diagrams opposite.

Arranging the Buffet Table

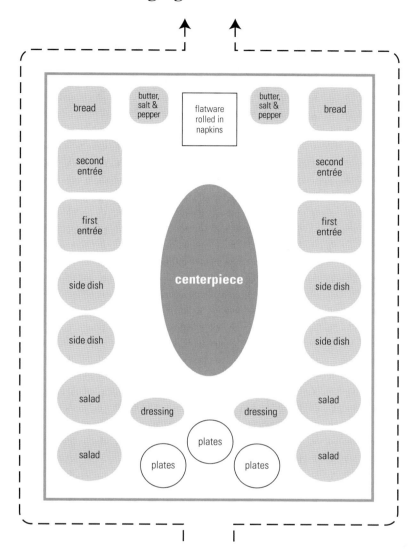

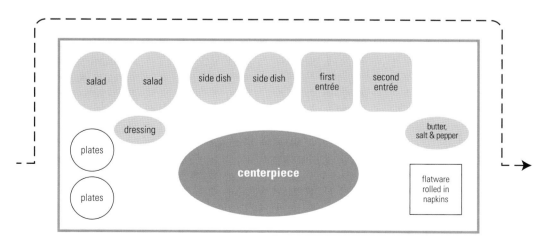

- **Table placement.** A buffet table that's close to the kitchen is easier to replenish. Keep in mind the flow of traffic in your house; separating the bar area from the buffet table will help prevent a bottleneck in traffic. When you have the space, a floating buffet table allows guests to access it from both sides; otherwise, the buffet table can be placed against a wall.

- **Centerpieces.** A centerpiece will help pull together the look of your buffet and can reflect your party's theme. Fresh flowers are a classic choice, but potted flowering plants can be grouped to create a centerpiece that you can repurpose later, perhaps as party favors. In fact, fun centerpieces can be created with many different types of party favors (see page 250 for favor ideas). For a gorgeous glow on your table, include classic taper candles or more modern arrangements of floating candles or pillar candles in varying heights. For more centerpiece ideas, see page 240.

- **Food.** While buffets are typically full meals with a salad, bread, an entrée or two and a side dish, they don't have to be complicated. Choose food that's easy to serve and eat (no crab legs, for instance), keeping in mind that guests will be filling their plates, carrying them to another location and likely eating out of their laps. Be sure all serving utensils and spoon rests are on the table ahead of time to keep things moving and neat. Coasters make convenient spoon rests.

- **Plates, napkins and flatware.** Plates need to be at the beginning of the buffet, for obvious reasons, but place the napkins, flatware and any condiments at the very end of the buffet, giving guests fewer items to balance as they make their way down the table. Flatware rolled up in napkins and tied closed (as in the napkin fold on page 40) makes for a user-friendly presentation that can be picked up at the end of the line.

- **Mix it up.** Create visual interest on your buffet by using serving dishes of varying heights, such as footed dishes and tiered servers. You can also build height by using risers underneath the tablecloth; just be sure to secure them to the table with tape. Keep hot dishes at table level to prevent spills. Varying textures and colors also add interest to the table. Use a woven basket to serve bread or crackers, a clear crystal bowl to show off a colorful salad and earthenware for a baked casserole. Try to reflect your party's theme in the choices you make; while it can be fun to play with accent colors, it can look very elegant to dress the table in a unified color scheme, such as varying shades of white or yellow (see photo, page 338).

25 Fabulous Table Settings

My book *The Entertaining Encyclopedia* contains 25 theme menus with delicious recipes for fun, low-stress parties. Here, I present ideas for beautiful table settings that are the perfect complement to each menu — or a similar theme menu of your own creation. I've even included some additional recipes to round out your meal.

There's a gorgeous table setting here for any occasion and venue, from a picnic to a champagne and caviar party, from a birthday shindig to a games night. Other cultures and cuisines provide endless inspiration for both table settings and food. You'll find suggestions for color palettes, decorations, centerpieces and party favors — and, of course, napkin folds! Let these ideas and the accompanying photographs inspire you to create your own fabulous themes and table settings!

Garden Brunch

Whether you host brunch in a sunroom or outside on a pretty patio, reflect the woodsy theme of this fresh springtime party in your tabletop decor, pulling in seasonal organic elements that you can collect from your own backyard (such as the spiky brown balls that fall from sweet gum trees), as well as plates and napkins that give a nod to the natural world. Garden gloves in a variety of colors make a fitting favor for this brunch; tie them together with a pretty ribbon and place a pair at each place.

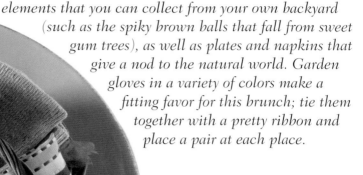

Napkin Folds

For a mixed crowd, try the Simple Upright fold (page 96), decorated with a bird design decal. Delight a group that includes children with the Bird's Nest (page 32), topped with a decorative bird from a craft store. The Diagonal fold (page 136) makes an elegant all-purpose choice, while the Shawl (page 176) is a cozy choice for a ladies' brunch, such as a wedding shower or book group. A bread basket can be outfitted with the Liner fold (page 70) to hold warm pastries or rolls.

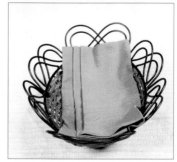

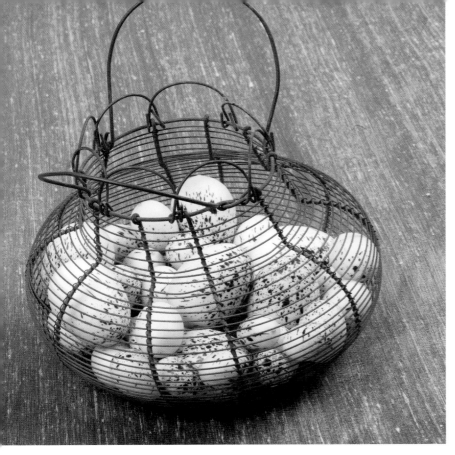

Color Palette

Accent a bare wooden table with cool shades of robin's egg blue and sage green balanced by warm creams, yellows, oranges and browns that evoke a natural feel; mix up textures with wire baskets and woven placemats or chargers.

For a complete menu of recipes that are perfect for a Garden Brunch, see *The Entertaining Encyclopedia*, page 292.

Arugula Almond Pesto

Makes 12 servings

1 tbsp	extra virgin olive oil	15 mL
1	head garlic, cloves peeled and coarsely chopped	1
12 oz	whole almonds	375 g
1 cup	loosely packed arugula	250 mL
¾ cup	extra virgin olive oil (approx.)	175 mL
	Grated zest of 1 lemon	
½ cup	freshly squeezed lemon juice (or to taste)	125 mL
	Sea salt and freshly ground black pepper	

1. In a skillet, heat 1 tbsp (15 mL) oil over medium-low heat. Sauté garlic for 7 minutes or until light golden. Transfer to a food processor.

2. Working in batches if necessary, add almonds, arugula, ¾ cup (175 mL) oil and lemon juice to food processor. Process, stopping to scrape down sides of bowl from time to time and adding more oil if necessary, until mixture resembles a thin paste.

3. Transfer to a bowl and season to taste with salt and pepper. Stir in lemon zest.

4. Cover and refrigerate for up to 2 days. Bring to room temperature before serving.

Tip: Use this pesto on grilled chicken breasts or tossed with pasta.

Picnic Boxed Lunch

Take the party outside to a scenic site and enjoy a casual picnic lunch or dinner with friends. Decorate invitations with pressed flowers or grasses, or use a rubber stamp to imprint cards with wildlife or ants. To set the scene, go to the picnic area early and hang brightly colored tissue paper flowers from the trees, bushes, porch or fence. Milk bottles filled with lemon slices, water and gerbera daisies make great centerpieces for spots with picnic tables.

Napkin Folds

Pack an individual lunch box for every guest and use the Tie One On fold (page 110) to attach a pretty cloth napkin, in contrasting colors, to each lunch box. If you opt to use dishes instead of lunch boxes, place each plate on an individual tray and use the Tie One On fold on the tray handle; it's an ideal napkin design for a picnic, as it won't blow away. You could also use The Standard fold (page 104), with either cloth or paper napkins.

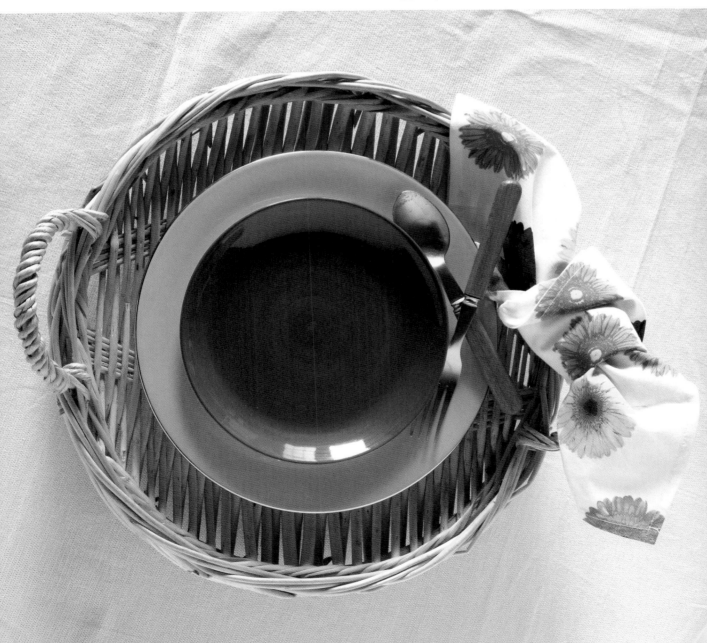

Color Palette

Collect inexpensive lunch boxes that will double as favors, in such brilliant colors as watermelon pink, fiery red, bright aqua and cool cobalt blue. As an alternative to serving the meal from lunch boxes, fill your picnic basket with pretty dishes in the same vivid hues.

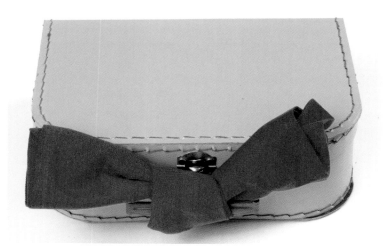

For a complete menu of recipes that are perfect for a Picnic Boxed Lunch, see *The Entertaining Encyclopedia,* page 298.

Brown Sugar–Chocolate Chip Cookies

Makes 24 cookies

- Preheat oven to 350°F (180°C)
- 2 baking sheets, greased

2 cups	packed dark brown sugar	500 mL
1/4 cup	granulated sugar	60 mL
2 cups	all-purpose flour	500 mL
1/2 tsp	baking soda	2 mL
1/2 tsp	salt	2 mL
1/4 tsp	baking powder	1 mL
3/4 cup	unsalted butter, at room temperature	175 mL
1	egg	1
1	egg yolk	1
2 tsp	vanilla extract	10 mL
2 cups	semisweet chocolate chips	500 mL
1 cup	chopped pecans	250 mL

1. In a small bowl, combine brown sugar and granulated sugar. Set aside.

2. In a medium bowl, whisk together flour, baking soda, salt and baking powder. Set aside.

3. In a large bowl, using an electric mixer on medium-high speed, beat butter until creamy. Beat in sugar mixture until light and fluffy. Beat in egg until well blended. Beat in egg yolk and vanilla until smooth, scraping down bowl as necessary. Using a wooden spoon, stir in flour mixture until just combined. Gently fold in chocolate chips and pecans.

4. Place dough by rounded tablespoons (15 mL) about 3 inches (7.5 cm) apart on prepared baking sheets. Bake in preheated oven for 10 minutes or until golden brown. Let cool for 10 minutes on baking sheets, then transfer to a wire rack to cool completely.

Tip: These cookies can be made up to 5 days ahead. Store in an airtight container at room temperature.

Kids' Treasure Hunt

Invite the kids to this pirate-themed party with invitations decorated with a treasure map, getting them excited for the main activity: a treasure hunt! For party favors, decorate small canvas tote bags with iron-on skull and crossbones designs — perfect for helping little pirates carry their loot. Enliven the tabletop with pirate-themed items arranged as a centerpiece: a weathered buccaneer's hat, a message in a bottle, coral and shells, gold coins or jewels and even a tissue paper parrot.

Napkin Folds

Set each place with a black, red or pirate-themed bandana positioned as a diamond-shaped placemat, or use black, white or red bandanas to create Placemat folds (page 76). Use the Loot Bag fold (page 72), made with another bandana and filled with chocolate gold coins, as a tabletop party favor at each place.

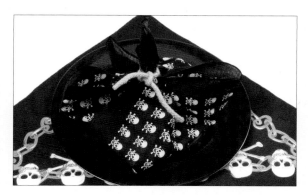

Color Palette

Black and white echo the Jolly Roger pirate flag, with its menacing skull and crossbones design, and bright red accents evoke the pirate's red bandana. Shades of sea green and blue bring to mind the ocean. Don't forget the metallic gold of doubloons and the worn wood of a treasure chest.

For a complete menu of recipes that are perfect for a Kids' Treasure Hunt, see *The Entertaining Encyclopedia*, page 304.

Candy Corn Cereal Mix

Makes 6 servings

2 cups	corn cereal squares	500 mL
1 cup	semisweet chocolate chips	250 mL
½ cup	candy corn	125 mL
½ cup	gum drops	125 mL

1. In a medium bowl, combine cereal, chocolate chips, candy corn and gum drops.

Neighborhood Block Party

Held on a gorgeous summer day with the great outdoors as your backdrop, a block party doesn't need much in the way of decor. It can be as simple as a color scheme carried through from hand-delivered invitations to the streamers and balloons used to decorate your deck, front porch or other party area. For the easiest in utensils, purchase disposable flatware — either individually wrapped kits or biodegradable forks and knives (such as those at www.webstaurantstore. com) — and place them, along with a color-coordinated napkin, in a plastic drink cup or beverage cozy, which can double as a take-home favor. Here, I used pencil holders with a fun lawn chair–like design, which makes them perfect summery beverage holders.

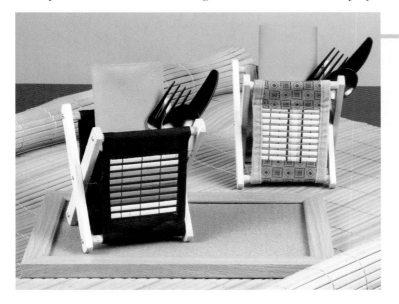

Napkin Folds

If you opt for cloth napkins, use the Buffet Roll (page 40), Ring Roll (page 86) or Pocket fold (page 80). They're all easy presentations that lend a casual air and on-the-go convenience to a block party. If using the Pocket fold for anything other than a sit-down meal, be sure to tie it together with ribbon or yarn to keep the napkin and flatware in one easy-to-grab unit.

Color Palette

The color trio of red, white and blue makes a fitting color scheme for summertime picnics held on or near Memorial Day or the Fourth of July. Red and white are the obvious choices for Canada Day. Glass-bottle green and dried-bamboo tan make a natural combination with modern flair, perfect for a block party any other summer weekend.

For a complete menu of recipes that are perfect for a Neighborhood Block Party, see *The Entertaining Encyclopedia*, page 308.

Jalapeño Cheese Corn Muffins

Makes 12 muffins

- Preheat oven to 400°F (200°C)
- 12-cup muffin pan, greased or lined with paper liners

2 cups	cornmeal	500 mL
2 cups	all-purpose flour	500 mL
1/4 cup	granulated sugar	60 mL
1 tbsp	baking powder	15 mL
1 tsp	salt	5 mL
4	eggs, lightly beaten	4
2 cups	buttermilk	500 mL
1/2 cup	butter, melted	125 mL
3	jalapeño peppers, seeded and minced	3
1 1/2 cups	shredded Cheddar cheese, divided	375 mL

1. In a large bowl, whisk together cornmeal, flour, sugar, baking powder and salt.

2. In another large bowl, whisk together eggs, buttermilk and butter until well combined. Stir in cornmeal mixture until just combined. Gently fold in jalapeños and 1 cup (250 mL) of the cheese.

3. Spoon batter into prepared muffin cups, dividing evenly. Sprinkle with the remaining cheese.

4. Bake in preheated oven for 25 minutes or until a tester inserted in the center of a muffin comes out clean. Let cool in pans on a wire rack for 5 minutes, then transfer to the rack to cool.

Tip: Make these muffins the day before and reheat in a 300°F (150°C) oven for 12 minutes before serving.

Birthday for a Special Mom

Decide on a feminine motif that best suits the guest of honor — hearts, flowers or a queen's crown, for instance — and use it on everything from the invitations to the tabletop decor to the garnish on the cake. Create centerpieces from flowers and greenery; fresh and silk can be combined for a lush, realistic-looking arrangement, and wired butterflies or other designs from the floral department of a crafts store can be tucked in too. Purchase heart- or flower-shaped placemats, or fashion them from tissue paper or fabric. A single fresh flower at each place, tied with a ribbon bearing the guest's name, doubles as favor and place card. Alternatively, choose a pretty pin for each guest to wear during the party.

Napkin Folds

For a royal look, use the Pope's Hat fold (page 82) in a deep color, accented with a pretty pin that doubles as a favor. The Heart fold (page 150) shows the guest of honor how much you love her, as does the Bouquet fold (page 34), which looks fresh in a modern floral print. The sophisticated Tropics fold (page 224) is perfect for an elegant affair.

Color Palette

Consider both the guest of honor's favorite colors and what works best with your established theme: rich magenta, pretty pink or summery shades of yellow make the decor feel feminine. White or cream table linens always make an elegant backdrop for colorful flowers or other accents.

Lemon Raspberry Birthday Cake

Makes 12 servings

- Preheat oven to 350°F (180°C)
- Two 8-inch (20 cm) round cake pans, greased

For a complete menu of recipes that are perfect for a Birthday for a Special Mom, see *The Entertaining Encyclopedia*, page 314.

Cake

1	box (18-¼ oz/500 g) lemon cake mix	1
3	eggs	3
⅓ cup	vegetable oil	75 mL

Buttercream Frosting

½ cup	shortening	125 mL
½ cup	unsalted butter, at room temperature	125 mL
2 tsp	vanilla extract	10 mL
4 cups	confectioners' (icing) sugar	1 L
2 tbsp	whole milk	25 mL
½ cup	raspberry jam	125 mL
1½ cups	sliced almonds	375 mL
	Edible dark pink flowers and greenery, for decorating	

1. **Cake:** Cut circles of parchment paper to fit in the bottom of each cake pan. Grease parchment paper. Dust all surfaces generously with flour. Invert cake pans over sink and tap out excess flour. Set aside.

2. In a large bowl, using cake mix, eggs, oil and 1 cup (250 mL) water, make batter according to package directions. Divide batter between cake pans.

3. Bake in preheated oven for 30 minutes or until a tester inserted in the center of the cakes comes out clean. Let cool in pans on wire racks for 30 to 45 minutes.

4. Carefully remove cakes from pans, peeling off parchment paper, and place on a clean work surface. Using a long serrated knife, carefully slice across the top of each cake layer as necessary to make a level surface.

5. **Frosting:** In a large bowl, using an electric mixer, beat shortening and butter until well combined. Beat in vanilla. Sprinkle with confectioners' sugar, 1 cup (250 mL) at a time, beating well after each addition. Add milk, 1 tbsp (15 mL) at a time, beating after each addition, until frosting is soft and fluffy but still firm enough to hold a shape.

6. Place one cake layer on a cake dish. Spread raspberry jam over top. Place second cake layer on top. Spread frosting thickly over entire surface of cake, covering top and sides. Press almonds into sides of cake, covering evenly.

7. Store at a cool room temperature or refrigerate for up to 2 days. A few hours before serving, decorate with flowers and greenery.

Tip: If you don't plan to use the frosting right away, cover it tightly with plastic wrap and refrigerate for up to 2 weeks. Bring it to room temperature before using and use an electric mixer to beat it until soft and fluffy.

Afternoon Tea

Decorate the table for a prettily proper afternoon tea by combining elegance with organic elements. Place flowering herbs such as lavender in small cream pitchers and group them together as a fragrant centerpiece; use the same number of pitchers as you have guests and they can double as favors. Another fitting favor is a pretty teacup or mug filled with teabags and honey sticks or fancy sugared stir-sticks, wrapped up in tulle and ribbon. Serve fresh herbal tea in inexpensive French presses. For place cards, cut out butterfly shapes from cardstock, secure the bottom with a pastel binder clip and write a guest's name on each.

Napkin Folds

Anchor the Orchid 1 fold (page 160) in a water glass or glass mug, or place the Dutch Baby fold (page 210) atop each plate. The Two Points fold (page 118) looks its most formal in white or with a corner-monogrammed napkin, and it also shows off napkins with contrasting edges nicely. The Vase fold (page 122) can hold fresh herbs, fresh flowers or even place cards.

Color Palette

Butter yellow, periwinkle blue, lavender and pink — pastels of any color, in fact — make pretty additions to the tabletop for a sweet teatime. A white or cream tablecloth makes an elegant backdrop and is always in fashion.

For a complete menu of recipes that are perfect for an Afternoon Tea, see *The Entertaining Encyclopedia*, page 320.

Lavender Lemon Verbena Shortbread

Makes 32 cookies

- Preheat oven to 300°F (150°C)
- 2 baking sheets, lined with parchment paper

4 cups	all-purpose flour	1 L
1½ tbsp	finely chopped fresh lavender flowers	22 mL
1½ tbsp	finely chopped fresh lemon verbena	22 mL
1 tsp	sea salt	5 mL
1 cup	confectioners' (icing) sugar	250 mL
½ cup	granulated sugar, divided	125 mL
1 cup	unsalted butter, at room temperature	250 mL
	Lavender flowers (fresh or dried) or fresh lemon verbena leaves	

1. In a large bowl, whisk together flour, lavender, lemon verbena and salt.

2. In another large bowl, using an electric mixer on low speed, beat confectioners' sugar, ⅓ cup (75 mL) of the granulated sugar and butter until well combined. Using a wooden spoon, stir in flour mixture until dough resembles coarse cornmeal.

3. Gather dough into a ball and place on a lightly floured work surface. Knead briefly, just until dough comes together. Divide dough into 4 pieces and roll out into disks about ¾ inch (2 cm) thick. Place on prepared baking sheets. Score shallow cut marks into the top of each disk to make 8 wedges. Decorate the top of each wedge with a lavender flower or lemon verbena leaf. Sprinkle with the remaining granulated sugar.

4. Bake in preheated oven for 22 minutes or until light golden. Remove from heat and, following score lines, cut into wedges while still warm. Let cool on pans on a wire rack.

Tip: These make a lovely treat for guests to take home.

Champagne and Caviar Party

For this upscale cocktail party, set the expectations for a glittering celebration with the invitations, using a gold or silver metallic pen on nice white note cards. Polish all your fancy silver or borrow interesting pieces for a fun mix-and-match look. If your guests will be mingling the entire time, place favors in a glass or metallic bowl in a central place, such as on a buffet. A faux pearl bangle or lapel pin in a gold or silver organza bag dresses your guests up for the evening; a couple of truffles packed in gold or silver favor boxes make a delicious take-home.

Napkin Folds

For a fun, over-the-top presentation, use the Peacock fold (page 166) in each wineglass. The Two Tails fold (page 120) is a great choice for understated elegance, especially with a solid-color hemstitched napkin. The Clutch fold (page 44) can be set at each place or displayed on a buffet table for parties that are more about mingling than sitting.

Color Palette

Use sophisticated, rich tones of maroon, golden yellow and brown for the table linens. Incorporate luminous accents with mother-of-pearl-handled or silver serving pieces, silver or gold chargers and gold or silver favor bags or boxes.

Types of Champagne

For a complete menu of recipes that are perfect for a Champagne and Caviar Party, see *The Entertaining Encyclopedia*, page 326.

Champagne signals celebration: serve sparkling wine in elegant glasses, and there's no doubt that you'll be toasting someone or something. When shopping for Champagne, it helps to remember that, technically, Champagne is sparkling wine from the Champagne region in France. California produces plenty of sparkling white wines made using the traditional method; look for "Méthode Champenoise" on the label.

A sparkling wine certainly doesn't have to be Champagne to be worthy of serving at a party: Spain's Cava and Italy's Prosecco offer good values that your guests will love. Italy's Asti Spumante is a sweeter sparkling white wine that can be served as a dessert wine.

Among the styles of Champagne are blanc de blancs, a light sparkling wine made with Chardonnay grapes; blanc de noirs, made with red grapes (Pinot Noir, Pinot Meunier or both); and rosé Champagne, which has some Pinot Noir added to give it its rosy hue, making it a fun choice for romantic occasions.

Because sparkling wine can range from very dry to very sweet, making it suitable as anything from a dry aperitif before the meal to a sweet dessert wine for afterwards, check the label for one of the following designations (listed here in order from driest to sweetest): brut, extra dry, sec, demi-sec or doux.

Types of Caviar

Caviar technically refers to salted sturgeon roe (eggs), though the term is often applied to other types of roe. An elegant appetizer, caviar is usually served in small quantities in simple presentations: on dainty pieces of toast, sometimes garnished with crème fraîche or sour cream. It can also be used to top deviled eggs or other bite-size appetizers. Because caviar is so expensive (and not everyone likes it), consider presenting it as an optional topping, setting it out in a small bowl nestled in a larger bowl of ice (it is extremely perishable).

Avoid the pressed version of caviar, which can be composed of several different types of eggs, usually damaged, and the pasteurized version, which has a different taste and texture than fresh. When you see "malossol" on the label, that means it has less salt. Here are the types to look for, all from Caspian Sea sturgeon, imported from Russia or Iran:

- **Beluga:** Considered the best caviar (and certainly the most expensive), beluga has extra-large, pea-size grains. It's delicate and soft, and it ranges from silver-gray to black in color.
- **Osetra:** With medium-size grains and a nutty taste, this caviar can have a color anywhere from golden yellow to gray to brown.
- **Sevruga:** This caviar has smaller grains, a gray to black color and a buttery taste.

For a fraction of the price, you can purchase other types of roe that serve the same purpose, including lumpfish caviar (tiny, hard black eggs with a salty, fishy flavor), whitefish caviar (small, crisp, yellow-gold eggs), salmon caviar (medium to large eggs that range from orange to red) and trout caviar (firm, medium-grained golden eggs), among others.

Wine and Cheese Tasting

So simple, yet so chic and satisfying, a wine and cheese tasting is a great way to host a party without having to do much (if any) cooking. Copy a favorite wine label to use as the invitation. As favors for your guests, buy an assortment of small blank journals that can serve as logs for their wine-tasting notes. Other favor ideas include a small bottle of olive oil or fancy vinegar with a recipe attached, or a small book about cheeses or wines. Chalkboards or pieces of slate work well as cheeseboards — use chalk to write the name of each cheese on the board for a bistro look. Make an edible centerpiece with nuts in the shell and bunches of grapes in a variety of colors. In addition to a generous assortment of breads and crackers, dried fruits and roasted nuts make good accompaniments to cheese and wine.

Napkin Folds

Use the Vase fold (page 122) on a set table, tucking a flower or sprig of herbs into each. Try the Triple Layer fold (page 184) for a tidy napkin that can be arranged at each place or stacked on the buffet table or the Fleur de Lis fold (page 148) to bring continental style to each place setting.

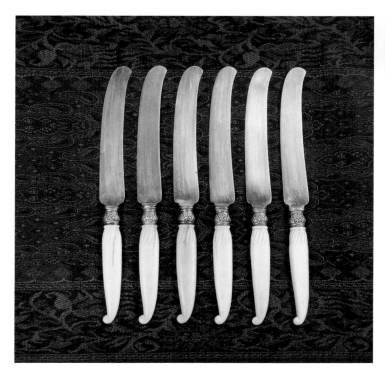

Color Palette

Use simple black chalkboards or warm wooden cutting boards for the cheese. Enliven the look with linens, china and other tabletop decor in shades of light to deep yellow, pale to punchy purple and natural olive green, accented with wine-inspired burgundy red.

For a complete menu of recipes that are perfect for a Wine and Cheese Tasting, see *The Entertaining Encyclopedia*, page 332.

Dessert Wines

A dessert wine is a sweeter, more full-flavored wine meant to be enjoyed after a meal or at the end of a wine tasting. Dessert wines are intended to be sipped and are commonly found in half-bottle sizes (making them excellent party favors!). There are three main types of dessert wines: late harvest, sauternes and ice wines.

Late harvest wines are made from grapes left longer on the vine. This causes more moisture evaporation, which results in higher levels of sugar. Germany produces many delicious late harvest wines, as do Washington and Oregon. They taste wonderful with fruit tarts or creamy desserts such as pudding, flan or crème brûlée.

Sauternes are among the finest wines in the world and are the result of a fungus called *Botrytis cinerea*, which causes the grape to lose moisture and shrivel up, making its sugar content very high. The most famous sauternes are from France, but Hungarian and German varieties are also delicious. Sauternes go well with coconut-, walnut- or banana-flavored desserts.

Ice wines are made from grapes that are allowed to stay on the vine so long that they freeze. Ice wines are generally not as sweet as sauternes but are sweeter than late harvest wines. They are right in the middle when it comes to price, too. Canada is the largest producer of ice wines. Pair ice wines with creamy desserts such as cheesecake, pudding, flans or crème brûlée.

Another option is to serve a fortified wine such as port or sherry alone or with dark chocolate desserts.

Girls' Night In

Have the book group over, watch a chick flick or just catch up in the comfort of your own home; at this party, it's ladies only. Spa themes are fun for groups of ladies; create small spa baskets as party favors. This is also the time to break out your favorite candy. Be girly, have fun and indulge!

Napkin Folds

The Clown Hat fold (page 132) is handy for hiding a small candy or favor at each place, and it's festive for grownups as well as for girls. The Bikini fold (page 28) is perfect for summer get-togethers, especially those that include a dip in the hot tub or pool. The Bouquet fold (page 34) works well with any theme; just choose a napkin and napkin ring that go with your color scheme.

Color Palette

Any combination of chocolate brown, lime green and pinks from light to bright will look feminine but unfussy, for modern-girl style. As always, use napkins that work well with your china, such as a multicolored citrus-print napkin paired with a yellow plate.

Tart au Fromage

Makes 6 to 10 servings

- Food processor
- 10-inch (25 cm) glass or metal pie plate

For a complete menu of recipes that are perfect for a Girls' Night In, see *The Entertaining Encyclopedia*, page 336.

Pie Crust

1 cup + 1½ tbsp	all-purpose flour	250 mL + 22 mL
½ tsp	salt	2 mL
½ tsp	granulated sugar	2 mL
¼ cup	cold unsalted butter, cut into small pieces	60 mL
2 tbsp	ice water (approx.)	30 mL

Filling

6	eggs, at room temperature	6
1 cup	whole milk	250 mL
⅔ cup	crème fraîche	150 mL
½ tsp	salt	2 mL
¼ tsp	freshly ground black pepper	1 mL
Pinch	ground nutmeg	Pinch
8 oz	Gruyère, Emmental or Swiss cheese, shredded	250 g

1. **Pie Crust:** In food processor, pulse flour, salt and sugar a few times to combine. Add butter and pulse until crumbly. Add ice water, 1 tbsp (15 mL) at a time, pulsing after each addition until a loose dough forms.

2. Form dough into a ball, then flatten into a disk. Wrap tightly in plastic wrap and refrigerate for at least 20 minutes or until chilled.

3. Roll out dough to fit pie plate. Trim and crimp edges. Using a fork, poke several holes in the bottom. Freeze for 30 minutes. Meanwhile, preheat oven to 425°F (220°C).

4. Line frozen pie dough with foil and fill with a cup of dried beans or pie weights. Bake for 15 minutes or until crust begins to brown. Remove foil and beans and bake for 7 minutes or until bottom begins to brown. Remove from oven, leaving oven on, and let cool.

5. **Filling:** In a large bowl, whisk together eggs, milk and crème fraîche. Whisk in salt, pepper and nutmeg. Stir in Gruyère. Pour into pie crust.

6. Bake for 30 minutes or until filling is golden and slightly puffy in the center. Let cool for 5 minutes before serving.

Tip: Plastic-wrapped dough can be stored in freezer bags in the freezer for up to 1 month. Let thaw in the refrigerator overnight before rolling.

Friends' Game Night

Host a game night for friends and the entertainment's all set. Let guests know what to expect with invitations decorated with images of playing cards, poker chips or Scrabble tiles. Leave tables clear for game-playing, setting the food up buffet-style on a sideboard or kitchen counter. Use a hole-punch to pierce playing cards and string them together to create a unique garland. Favors are easy: tie a ribbon around a new set of playing cards and add a tag with each guest's name, or purchase inexpensive kids' games or toys, such as Slinkys, sets of pick-up sticks or travel-size checkers.

Napkin Folds

Because the party games are likely to take over the dining-room table, set up the food as a buffet and use the Bouquet fold (page 34) or the Buffet Roll fold (page 40); both are held together with napkin rings or ribbons, so they can be piled in a basket and picked up at the end of the buffet.

Color Palette

Mimic the colors in a deck of cards by using black, white and red. Playing cards themselves can serve as place cards, embellishments for invitations and even garlands. Add bright lime green as a modern contrast.

For a complete menu of recipes that are perfect for a Friends' Game Night, see *The Entertaining Encyclopedia*, page 340.

Walnut Dip

Makes 6 servings

2	zucchini, thinly sliced	2
1	clove garlic, roughly chopped	1
½	red onion, roughly chopped	½
¼ cup	loosely packed fresh flat-leaf (Italian) parsley leaves	60 mL
¼ cup	loosely packed fresh mint leaves	60 mL
¼ cup	chopped walnuts	60 mL
½ cup	sour cream	125 mL
2 tbsp	olive oil	30 mL
1 tbsp	freshly squeezed lemon juice	15 mL
¼ tsp	salt (or to taste)	1 mL

1. Place zucchini in a microwave-safe bowl. Cover with plastic wrap and microwave on High for 1 minute or until tender.

2. Transfer zucchini to a food processor or blender. Add garlic, red onion, parsley, mint, walnuts, sour cream, oil, lemon juice and salt; process until evenly ground but still a little chunky. Transfer to a bowl, cover and refrigerate until serving, for up to 1 day.

Tip: Serve with pita chips or crudités.

Oscar Night

I love to watch the Oscars with friends, and it's fun to have finger foods that can be enjoyed in front of the television but are a little bit fancy in honor of the swanky awards ceremony and after-parties. Among many other munchies, I like to include moviegoers' favorite snack — popcorn — since this is a night celebrating movies. Use paper or plastic movie theater–style tubs, available at World Market (www.worldmarket.com) or Target (www.target.com), to serve it. Have your friends place their votes on winners ahead of time, and have a door prize (or two) for the one with the most correct guesses.

Napkin Folds

You're more likely to be setting trays for this party than your dining-room table. Use the Clutch fold (page 44), making it into an envelope (like those that reveal the year's big-screen winners). Another option is the Tuxedo fold (page 186), in honor of the Hollywood finery on display; this fold offers each guest two napkins, which can come in handy when you're eating away from the table.

Color Palette

Black and white, the classic tuxedo combination, is an elegant ode to the Oscars. Don't forget red for the red carpet and metallic gold for those sought-after statuettes.

Truffled Popcorn

Makes 6 servings

¼ cup	unsalted butter, melted	60 mL
1 tsp	truffle oil	5 mL
8 cups	freshly popped popcorn	2 L
1 tsp	fine sea salt (or to taste)	5 mL

1. In a small bowl, combine butter and truffle oil.

2. Place popcorn in a large bowl. Drizzle with butter mixture and toss to coat. Season with salt. Serve hot.

For a complete menu of recipes that are perfect for an Oscar Night party, see *The Entertaining Encyclopedia*, page 344.

Super Bowl Party

You don't have to be a football fan to throw a terrific Super Bowl party; it's all about getting together with friends for casual food and conversation — and to watch the game, of course. Decorate invitations with team colors, encourage guests to wear their team gear and carry the theme through to your decor with hanging pennants and a basket of Nerf footballs, which make for halftime fun as well as favors (write each guest's name on a football).

Color Palette

Evoke the feeling of being at the game with bright Astroturf green, the dark brown of a football and the bright blue of the sky. Pull in team colors, too — especially if most of your crowd is loyal to the same side.

Napkin Folds

Tie the Cup Kerchief fold (page 48) around big mugs or bowls for chili. Or try the Buffet Roll fold (page 40), wrapping up the chili spoon and napkin in one neat package for guests to pick up at the end of the buffet.

For a complete menu of recipes that are perfect for a Super Bowl Party, see *The Entertaining Encyclopedia*, page 350.

Chili Con Carne

Makes 8 servings

1 tbsp	olive oil	15 mL
1 cup	chopped onion	250 mL
2 lbs	lean ground turkey	1 kg
2	cans (each 14 to 19 oz/398 to 540 mL) red, pinto or kidney beans, drained and rinsed	2
2	cans (each 28 oz/796 mL) crushed tomatoes	2
2 to 4 tbsp	chili powder (or to taste)	30 to 60 mL
	Salt and freshly ground black pepper	
1 to 2 tsp	cider vinegar (optional)	5 to 10 mL
	Chopped red onion, tomato and cilantro	
	Shredded Cheddar cheese	

1. In a large pot, heat oil over medium-high heat. Sauté onion for 5 minutes or until softened. Add turkey and cook, breaking it up with the back of a spoon, for 6 minutes or until no longer pink.

2. Stir in beans, crushed tomatoes and chili powder, salt and pepper to taste; bring to a boil. Reduce heat and simmer, stirring occasionally, for 20 minutes.

3. Remove from heat and stir in vinegar to taste (if using). Serve with bowls of red onion, tomato, cilantro and cheese for garnishing.

Backyard Campout

With a backyard campout, the setting is the attraction, so there's very little decorating to do. Pitch a tent, bring out the lawn furniture and picnic blankets and, if your area allows it (or you have a permit), build a little fire in a fire pit. Guests will bring their own camping gear; you'll simply provide the setting and the food, with the ease of being steps from your kitchen rather than really out on the trails. To make the under-the-stars memories last, offer guests a jar of colorful beans with your favorite bean soup recipe attached — perhaps mine?

Napkin Folds

No napkin folds are necessary when you're roughing it; simply hang colorful cloth napkins, kitchen towels or bandanas from the backyard fence.

Color Palette

Burlap brown, barn red, grass green and bright sky blue echo the great outdoors and fit right in; use enamel campware dishes in one or more of those shades and echo those colors in your napkin decorations.

For a complete menu of recipes that are perfect for a Backyard Campout, see *The Entertaining Encyclopedia*, page 356.

Mixed Bean Soup

Makes 6 servings

1 tbsp	olive oil	15 mL
1 tbsp	butter	15 mL
2	onions, chopped	2
2	stalks celery, sliced	2
2	cloves garlic, minced	2
1	large carrot, cut in half lengthwise and sliced	1
1	can (28 oz/796 mL) crushed tomatoes	1
6 cups	reduced-sodium chicken broth	1.5 L
1 cup	rinsed drained canned red kidney beans	250 mL
1 cup	rinsed drained canned white kidney beans	250 mL
1/2 cup	rinsed drained canned black beans	125 mL
1/2 cup	rinsed drained canned chickpeas	125 mL
2	sprigs fresh thyme	2
2	sprigs fresh flat-leaf (Italian) parsley	2
	Salt and freshly ground black pepper	

1. In a large saucepan, heat oil and butter over medium-high heat. Sauté onions for 5 minutes or until softened. Add celery, garlic and carrot; sauté for 5 minutes.

2. Stir in tomatoes, broth, red kidney beans, white kidney beans, black beans, chickpeas, thyme, parsley and salt and pepper to taste; bring to a boil. Reduce heat and simmer for 30 minutes to blend the flavors. Discard thyme and parsley.

Southern Charm

Folks take warm hospitality and decadent party food very seriously in the Deep South, so it's a fitting inspiration for a party — one that will make guests feel very well attended to. Pull in botanical elements from the herb garden for the invitations, using a dried sprig of lavender for muted color and scent. Clustered small pots of lavender make a great centerpiece and can serve as take-home favors. The fragrant herb of the day also flavors the iced tea (see recipe, page 311). Yellow roses, a symbol of friendship, are another good choice that can be carried through from the invitations to the tabletop.

Napkin Folds

Use the Herb Pot fold (page 152) atop each plate for a pretty luncheon, tucking fresh herbs or a flower into each. The Fleur fold (page 146), prepared with a smaller napkin, is another nice choice for daytime entertaining, such as a luncheon or tea. The Shield fold (page 94) and Two Points fold (page 118) are simple, elegant choices for lunch or dinner, especially with a white or solid-color hemstitched napkin.

Color Palette

Garden inspiration comes from flowering lavender, lemon yellow and leaf green; highlight these relatively muted natural colors by keeping the backdrop simple with a white tablecloth or bare wood table.

For a complete menu of recipes that are perfect for a Southern Charm party, see *The Entertaining Encyclopedia*, page 360.

Lavender-Mint Iced Tea

Makes 6 servings

4	mint tea bags	4
3	lavender tea bags	3
2 cups	boiling water	500 mL
¾ cup	liquid honey	175 mL
4 cups	cold water	1 L
	Fresh lavender or mint sprigs	

1. Place mint and lavender tea bags in a heatproof 2-quart (2 L) pitcher and pour in boiling water. Let steep for 4 minutes, then remove tea bags and discard. Stir in honey until dissolved. Add cold water and refrigerate until chilled.

2. To serve, pour tea over ice and garnish with a lavender or mint sprig.

Western Hoedown

This casual cookout has Western flair. Let your guests in on the theme with invitations that use images of hay bales, cowboys or farm animals. Keep the decor for the party fresh (and reusable) by piling lemons or limes in small wood crates or baskets. Fashion simple flower arrangements from aluminum cans covered with gingham fabric and filled with sunflowers or daisies. As a favor at each place, give guests their own barbecue mop; give kids a small collection of plastic farm animals to play with.

Napkin Folds

Use the Hobo Sack fold (page 68) if you're including a favor that will fit neatly inside it, such as a small game or toy that will keep kids (and the young at heart) happily occupied. The Pocket fold (page 80) is another natural choice for this party. For either fold, use gingham fabric or a bandana.

Color Palette

Lemon yellow and lime green keep the color scheme fresh and updated; barn red and deep sky blue evoke country life, especially in Western or country-style prints.

For a complete menu of recipes that are perfect for a Western Hoedown, see *The Entertaining Encyclopedia*, page 368.

BBQ Sauce

Makes 2 cups (500 mL)

2 cups	ketchup	500 mL
⅓ cup	light (fancy) molasses	75 mL
1 tbsp	packed brown sugar	15 mL
2 tbsp	liquid honey	30 mL
2 tbsp	Worcestershire sauce	30 mL
1½ tbsp	cider vinegar	22 mL
1 tbsp	Dijon mustard	15 mL
¼ tsp	cayenne pepper	1 mL

1. In a medium saucepan, combine ketchup, molasses, brown sugar, honey, Worcestershire sauce, vinegar, mustard and cayenne; heat over medium heat, stirring until sugar is dissolved. Increase heat and bring to a boil. Reduce heat and simmer, stirring frequently, for 15 minutes or until thickened. Let cool to room temperature.

2. Transfer to an airtight container and refrigerate for up to 5 days.

Pacific Northwest Coast

Use seashells to give your tabletop a coastal feel. Larger shells can serve as place cards; use a metallic paint pen to write a guest's name on each. For the centerpiece, arrange a flowing length of ocean-colored fabric, mound sand in the center and scatter seashells atop it; you can even add seashell-shaped candles. Or fill a large container with sand and arrange pillar candles inside, in varying sizes and seaside shades, bringing a soft glow to the dining room. If your table is wood, use chargers instead of a tablecloth, bringing more rustic beauty to the setting by letting the wood show.

Napkin Folds

Use the Clamshell fold (page 208) for an impressive dinner party presentation. When the party includes children, make whimsical little boats with the Sailboat fold (page 92). Try the Wave fold (page 192) for a fun way to incorporate the flatware.

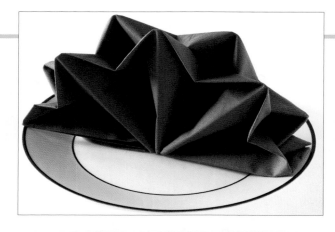

Color Palette

Summon the cool beauty of the Pacific Northwest in shades of slate gray, dark blue, sea green and teal; warm it up with natural tones of cream and browns.

For a complete menu of recipes that are perfect for a Pacific Northwest Coast party, see *The Entertaining Encyclopedia*, page 374.

Salmon Chowder with Dill

Makes 6 servings

6	slices thick-cut bacon, chopped	6
2	stalks celery, thinly sliced	2
1	red onion, finely chopped	1
1	leek (white and light green parts only), thinly sliced	1
2	red-skinned potatoes, diced	2
3 cups	whole milk	750 mL
½ cup	heavy or whipping (35%) cream	125 mL
1½ lbs	skinless salmon fillet (preferably wild-caught), cut into 1-inch (2.5 cm) pieces	750 g
	Salt and freshly ground black pepper	
¼ cup	loosely packed fresh dill	60 mL
1	lemon, cut into 6 wedges	1

1. In a large saucepan, over medium-high heat, cook bacon until crisp. Using a slotted spoon, transfer to a plate lined with paper towels to drain.

2. Add celery, red onion and leek to fat remaining in skillet; sauté for 8 minutes or until light golden. Add potatoes and sauté for 3 minutes. Add milk and cream; bring to a boil, stirring constantly. Reduce heat and simmer, stirring often, until potatoes are tender. Add salmon and cook for 3 minutes or until fish flakes easily when tested with a fork. Remove from heat and stir in bacon and dill. Season to taste with salt and pepper. Serve with lemon wedges.

Hawaiian Luau

It's easy for guests to feel relaxed when the party's a mellow Hawaiian luau, complete with umbrella drinks. Gather tropical fruits like whole pineapples, mangos, papayas, limes and star fruit for a centerpiece that overflows with tropical colors and flavors. Large tropical leaves make a vibrant addition to the tabletop; anchor one underneath each dinner plate, fanning it out to one side. Immerse a few orchid blooms in water inside tall, clear glass vases. Choose napkins in solid tropical shades or in Hawaiian-print fabrics. As guests arrive, give each a silk lei to wear for the party — and to wear home.

Napkin Folds

When you're ready to party island-style, use the funky Aloha Shirt fold (page 202). The spiky Bird of Paradise fold (page 206) makes a striking statement. The understated Simply Skinny fold (page 100) works for nearly any occasion; dress it up for this party with a tropical flower.

Color Palette

Shades borrowed from tropical fruits like pineapple, mango, papaya and lime — and the hot hues of island flowers, such as magenta bougainvillea — can be cooled off by the bright blue of island water and the bright green of tropical foliage.

For a complete menu of recipes that are perfect for a Hawaiian Luau, see *The Entertaining Encyclopedia*, page 380.

Easy Pineapple Granita

Makes 6 servings

1	pineapple, peeled, cored and chopped	1
2 cups	lime- or lemon-flavored yogurt	500 mL
1 cup	sweetened shredded coconut	250 mL
	Lime wedges	

1. Spread pineapple in a single layer on a baking sheet and freeze for at least 2 hours, until solid, or for up to 3 days.

2. Working in batches if necessary, place frozen pineapple and yogurt in a food processor or blender and blend until smooth. Add coconut and pulse briefly just to combine.

3. Spoon into dessert glasses and serve with lime wedges.

Mexican Fiesta

There's something inherently festive and universally loved about Mexican food, so it makes a great basis for a party menu for many different occasions. Sombreros, cacti or chile peppers are a good design element to carry through from invitations to decor to favors. A soft straw hat makes an original chip and dip server: place a hat in the center of the table, line the crown with a colorful cloth napkin and place a bowl of salsa inside, then fill the brim with blue and white corn tortilla chips.

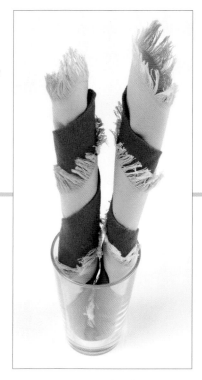

Napkin Folds

Use the Burro fold (page 42) for messier meals, as it includes two napkins per guest; it will work with a buffet, too, because it's placed in beer glasses (or tie it with twine). Other choices could be the fanciful Parrot fold (page 164) atop each plate or the Pleat fold (page 78) as a more understated way to show off a fun border-striped fabric.

Color Palette

Bring south-of-the-border heat to the table with vibrant shades of orange, yellow and red, with saturated hues of blue and turquoise to cool things down. Add straw hats, chargers or baskets for extra texture.

For a complete menu of recipes that are perfect for a Mexican Fiesta, see *The Entertaining Encyclopedia*, page 386.

Mango Margarita

Makes 1 serving

• Blender

1½ cups	ice cubes	375 mL
½ cup	chopped mango (fresh or frozen)	125 mL
2 oz	tequila	60 mL
½ oz	Triple Sec	15 mL
2 tbsp	filtered water	30 mL

1. In a blender, blend ice cubes, mango, tequila, Triple Sec and filtered water until smooth. Pour into a margarita glass and serve.

Barcelona Bash

Host a sumptuous late-afternoon lunch, following Spanish tradition. The scent of saffron will mingle enticingly with spiced centerpieces when you fill oblong wooden bowls with fragrant clove-studded oranges and star anise. Pretty painted jugs and earthenware serving dishes contribute more Spanish country style. Be sure to set out dishes of marinated olives and salted Marcona almonds for guests to nibble on before the meal.

Napkin Folds

Use pretty wineglasses to show off the Duet fold (page 58), for a meal that merits two napkins per guest, or the Orchid 2 fold (page 218), with its softer, petal-like design. The Fish fold (page 144) is especially fun with brightly colored napkins, and the Stairway fold (page 178) reaches dramatic heights.

Color Palette

Look for rich earth tones, including the dark brown of rustic wood, enlivened with golden mustard yellow, citrusy orange, rust red and olive green.

For a complete menu of recipes that are perfect for a Barcelona Bash, see *The Entertaining Encyclopedia*, page 392.

Saffron Rice Pilaf

Makes 6 servings

1/4 cup	butter	60 mL
1	onion, chopped	1
1	clove garlic, minced	1
1 1/2 cups	long-grain white rice	375 mL
1/4 tsp	saffron threads (or 1/8 tsp/0.5 mL ground saffron)	1 mL
3 cups	reduced-sodium chicken broth	750 mL
1/2 cup	coarsely chopped almonds, toasted	125 mL
1/4 cup	chopped fresh flat-leaf (Italian) parsley	60 mL
2 tsp	grated orange zest	10 mL

1. In a medium saucepan, melt butter over medium heat. Sauté onion for 7 minutes or until golden. Add garlic and sauté for 2 minutes. Add rice and saffron, stirring well to coat rice in butter.

2. Stir in broth and bring to a boil. Reduce heat to low, cover and simmer for 20 minutes or until liquid is absorbed. Let stand, covered, for 5 minutes. Fluff with a fork, then stir in almonds, parsley and orange zest. Serve hot.

Italian Pasta Party

The olive tree is a symbol of peace and wisdom, and its fruit (and that fruit's oil) is a mainstay of Italian cuisine. What better image to extend on invitations to friends and family? Use the image of an olive tree, olive branch or olives on invitations and place cards, and carry the theme through with the favors, setting a small bottle of olive oil, perhaps with a favorite recipe attached, at each place. In November or December, bring a warm look of abundance to the table with centerpieces overflowing with sugared fruits, surrounded by pinecones and holiday ornaments.

Napkin Folds

Use the casually elegant Duet fold (page 58) for potentially messy spaghetti meals, as each guest will get two napkins. The Trifold (page 114), gathered and secured with a napkin ring or ribbon, works well for buffets. Either the Divided Square fold (page 54) or the Diamonds fold (page 50) would make for a streamlined arrangement atop each plate.

Color Palette

Evoke the rich, warm feel of Italian celebrations with dark orange, earthy brown, wine-colored reds and purples and olive green.

For a complete menu of recipes that are perfect for an Italian Pasta Party, see *The Entertaining Encyclopedia*, page 398.

Creating a Cheese Plate

A cheese plate is a smart addition to nearly any party. It can be served before dinner as an appetizer, as part of the spread for a cocktail party or cocktail supper, or after dinner with a fortified wine — and with very little effort. The only accompaniment needed is a variety of breads, but don't forget that dried and fresh fruits are natural pairings for cheese, too. And if you want to create a full-blown antipasti platter, simply add cured meats such as prosciutto or salami, marinated olives, artichoke hearts, sun-dried tomatoes and roasted peppers.

When assembling even the simplest cheese plate, include at least three types of cheese, offering variety in taste and texture, and perhaps in color. Look for a fresh unripened cheese, a blue cheese, a soft or semi-soft cheese and a firm or hard cheese. Take the time to ask the person working at your cheese shop or cheese counter for recommendations; he or she can help craft a cheese plate full of tastes and textures designed especially for your menu.

For an Italian party like this one, consider selecting all Italian cheeses: fresh mozzarella (bite-size marinated bocconcini is great for parties); Gorgonzola, Italy's earthy, pungent blue cheese; buttery fontina; and crumbly Parmigiano-Reggiano.

German Feast

Celebrate your favorite guy with a manly menu full of hearty wintertime fare worthy of the best Dunkel (dark) beer you can find. Use beer steins as a design element: put their image on invitations and use them as vases for a line of simple centerpiece flower arrangements. For favors, put together a mix-and-match six-pack of German beers for each couple; put the six-pack at one person's place and a package of paper beer coasters from around the world (available at www.worldmarket.com) at the other's. An assortment of gourmet mustards adds its own rich colors to the tabletop; small jars of special mustard would also make a great take-home favor.

Napkin Folds

Use the Luna Moth fold (page 216) or the Bird in Flight fold (page 30) to bring a bit of Bavarian whimsy to the table. The Two-Headed Fish fold (page 188) and Reveal fold (page 174) work well with two-sided napkins and offer more understated style atop each plate.

Color Palette

Bring a rustic but celebratory feel to the table with ceramic baking and serving dishes, china and table linens in cheery shades of bright orange and golden yellow, offset by the rich brown of wooden boards or tabletops and earthy rust reds.

Beer-Braised Sausages

Makes 6 servings

For a complete menu of recipes that are perfect for a German Feast, see *The Entertaining Encyclopedia*, page 404.

- Preheat oven to 325°F (160°C)
- Ovenproof Dutch oven

1 tbsp	olive oil	15 mL
1	large onion, thickly sliced	1
6	smoked Polish or kielbasa sausages	6
6 cups	German lager beer	1.5 L
12	whole black peppercorns	12
	Variety of German mustards	

1. In Dutch oven, heat oil over medium heat. Sauté onion for 10 minutes or until lightly browned. Add sausages and sauté for 3 minutes. Add beer and peppercorns; bring to a boil.

2. Cover and bake in preheated oven for 30 minutes. Using a slotted spoon, remove sausages and onions from braising liquid and place on a serving platter; discard liquid. Serve with a variety of German mustards.

Grecian Get-Together

Make your own marinated feta cheese to serve at the party and pack a small jar for each guest to take home as a delicious party favor. Miniature Greek columns found at crafts stores (usually in the wedding section) can be used to support place cards with classical style. Use all-white serving dishes in a variety of shapes and sizes for a striking look. Pull in any of a number of shades of blue in the table linens, from aqua to dark blue, to reflect the blue of the Aegean Sea, the sky or the Greek flag. Tuck sprigs of rosemary into the flower arrangements for a light fragrance that goes well with the meal.

Napkin Folds

Keep it simple with The Standard fold (page 104) or the Ring Roll fold (page 86), or add more angles of interest with the fun Pinwheel fold (page 168) or High Tower fold (page 154).

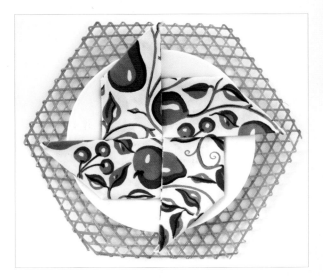

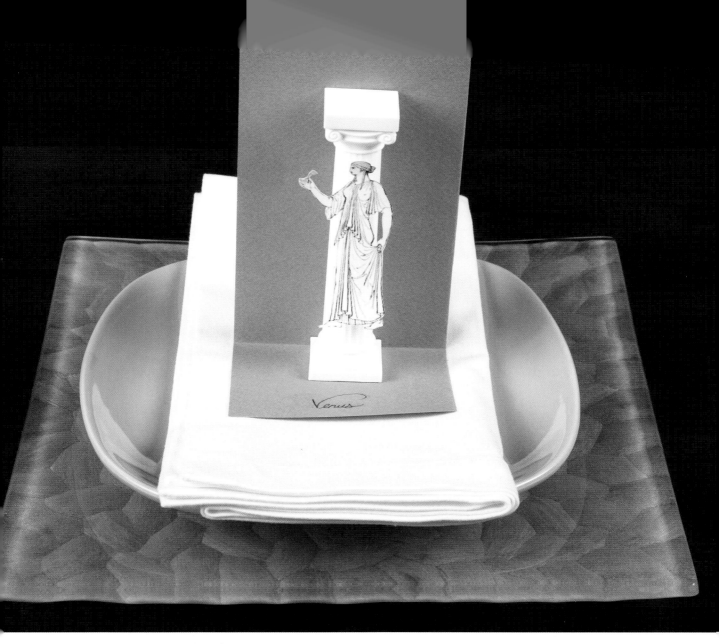

Color Palette

A simple color scheme of blue and white is perfectly in line with the Greek flag, and it evokes the country's white architectural treasures set against the bright blue sea and sky. Whites can range from bright to creamy, and blues can run from aqua to dark blue.

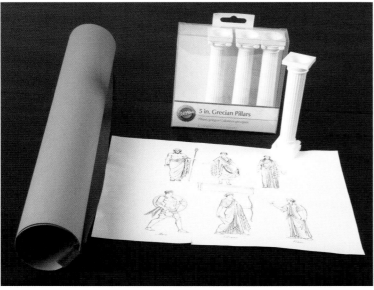

Buy or borrow serving plates in a variety of shapes and sizes but all in the same color. White or cream is the most versatile choice. This will give your table an eclectic yet pulled-together look that is very modern. Look for pieces on sale at stores like World Market, T.J Maxx Home Goods, Ross, Kohl's, Target and Home Sense.

For a complete menu
of recipes that are
perfect for a Grecian
Get-Together, see
*The Entertaining
Encyclopedia*, page 410.

Marinated Feta

Makes 6 servings

8 oz	feta cheese, drained and patted dry	250 g
1 tbsp	chopped fresh oregano (or 1 tsp/5 mL dried)	15 mL
1 tbsp	chopped fresh rosemary (or 1 tsp/5 mL dried)	15 mL
1 tsp	grated lemon zest	5 mL
1 tsp	grated orange zest	5 mL
1/8 tsp	hot pepper flakes (optional)	0.5 mL
12	whole black peppercorns	12
2 cups	extra virgin olive oil (approx.)	500 mL

1. Cut feta into ½-inch (1 cm) dice and place in a 3- to 4-cup (750 mL to 1 L) glass jar. Add oregano, rosemary, lemon zest, orange zest, hot pepper flakes and peppercorns. Add enough oil to just cover feta.

2. Cover and refrigerate for at least 2 days or for up to 1 week. Bring to room temperature before serving with crusty bread for dipping.

Turkish Twilight

The Turkish flag, which has a red background and a white crescent moon and star, can serve as inspiration for invitations and decor: keep moons, stars and a variety of rich jewel tones in mind as you pull together table settings and centerpieces. Silky textures add a luxurious look and feel, and beaded trims catch the light. Create favors by filling small organza bags with candies. Attach each guest's name to a bag with a ribbon, and the favor doubles as a place card. If you have a smaller dinner party planned, consider serving your guests around a large, low coffee table and seat them on cushions on the floor, for an intimate, relaxed setting.

Napkin Folds

The Duet fold (page 58) gives each guest two napkins, arranged together in a wineglass. Another elegant, wineglass-anchored fold is the Orchid 2 design (page 218), which has a more feminine, floral look. The Stairway fold (page 178) always makes a dramatic presentation, adding height to each place setting, while the Pope's Hat fold (page 82), embellished with a pretty star, is less showy but no less elegant.

Color Palette

Think rich jewel tones of red, purple, green and blue, accented with lustrous gold, bronze and brown. Fabrics with a silky sheen or beaded trim add texture and shine.

For a complete menu of recipes that are perfect for a Turkish Twilight party, see *The Entertaining Encyclopedia*, page 416.

Apricot Compote

Makes 6 servings

⅔ cup	granulated sugar	150 mL
12	apricots, peeled and sliced	12
1 tsp	almond extract	5 mL
¼ cup	sliced almonds, toasted	60 mL

1. In a medium saucepan, bring sugar and 4 cups (1 L) water to a boil over high heat. Reduce heat to medium-low and stir in apricots and almond extract; simmer for 8 minutes. Remove from heat and let cool.

2. Transfer to an airtight container and refrigerate for up to 1 week. Stir in almonds before serving.

Tip: The compote is delicious spooned over ice cream.

African Ivory Coast

When the occasion calls for something exotic, draw inspiration from Africa for a party that transports your guests. Create an easy centerpiece ripe with textures, colors and even scents by arranging papayas and limes, some halved, in a rustic basket. As a theme to carry through from the invitations to the tabletop, consider some of the continent's big, beautiful animals: elephants, zebras or giraffes. Widely available animal-print fabrics, paper products and gift items can add sass to the invitations, table settings and party favors.

Napkin Folds

Use the Divided Fan fold (page 52), tied with a shell or sand dollar attached, or use the Ring Roll fold (page 86) when you have pretty napkin rings you want to show off. The Gypsy Skirt fold (page 66) is a fun way to highlight cloth napkins with lively trim.

Color Palette

Natural safari-style shades of ivory, khaki, bronze and brown can be enlivened with more vibrant tones of orange, deep red and royal blue.

Mafe

Makes 8 servings

2 tbsp	vegetable oil (approx.)	30 mL
2 lbs	stewing beef	1 kg
1	large onion, finely chopped	1
4	cloves garlic, minced	4
1	1-inch (2.5 cm) piece gingerroot, minced	1
2 tbsp	tomato paste	30 mL
1	can (28 oz/796 mL) crushed tomatoes	1
2 cups	reduced-sodium chicken broth	500 mL
1 cup	reduced-sodium creamy peanut butter	250 mL
	Salt and freshly ground black pepper	
½ cup	unsalted roasted peanuts, coarsely chopped	125 mL

For a complete menu of recipes that are perfect for an African Ivory Coast party, see *The Entertaining Encyclopedia*, page 422.

1. In a large saucepan, heat half the oil over medium-high heat. Working in batches, cook beef for 5 minutes or until browned on all sides, adding oil as needed between batches. Using a slotted spoon, transfer beef to a bowl.

2. Add onion to saucepan and sauté for 7 minutes or until light golden. Add garlic and ginger; sauté for 3 minutes.

3. Return beef and any accumulated juices to saucepan and stir in tomato paste. Stir in tomatoes and broth; bring to a boil. Reduce heat and simmer, stirring occasionally, for 20 minutes.

4. Stir in peanut butter and salt and pepper to taste; simmer for 45 minutes or until beef is tender. Serve garnished with chopped peanuts.

Chinese Banquet

Don't be intimidated by the idea of hosting a Chinese banquet: you can pull off the party with as much or as little home cooking as you like. Present takeout on your own china or prepare the whole menu from scratch. Either way, fortune cookies are a must, as they make for fun party conversation. They can be served on their own or as a garnish atop ice cream or sorbet. For a more decadent dessert, dip them in chocolate. Images of dragons can grace invitations, place cards or a pretty table runner. Chinese knots made of red silk cord can serve as ties for napkins or as a decorative element to hang on place cards.

Napkin Folds

Use the Bowtie fold (page 38) as a way to present a cloth napkin and a pair of chopsticks in one neat package, or try the Divided Fan fold (page 52), tied with a decorative element such as a seashell or Chinese coin. The Fortune Cookie fold (page 64) holds place cards or handwritten fortunes, while the Fan fold (page 60) stays upright in a small bowl, teacup or takeout box.

Color Palette

Use understated ivory, black and brown as the mainstays of your decor, pulling in various textures by pairing glazed china with bamboo-handled flatware, basket-weave chargers or placemats made from sticks. Accent the muted palette with shiny lacquered red or jade green.

For a complete menu of recipes that are perfect for a Chinese Banquet, see *The Entertaining Encyclopedia*, page 428.

Sesame Asparagus

Makes 6 to 8 servings

2 tsp	white sesame seeds	10 mL
1 tsp	black sesame seeds	5 mL
1 tbsp	olive oil	15 mL
1½ lbs	asparagus (preferably thin spears), trimmed and cut into 2-inch (5 cm) pieces	750 g
	Salt and freshly ground black pepper	

1. In a large skillet, over medium heat, toast white and black sesame seeds, stirring frequently, for 2 minutes or until fragrant. Transfer to a small dish and set aside.
2. Increase heat to high and add oil to skillet. Cook asparagus, stirring frequently, for 5 to 7 minutes or until bright green and tender-crisp. Remove from heat and stir in sesame seeds. Season to taste with salt and pepper.

Library and Archives Canada Cataloguing in Publication

Vivaldo, Denise

    Perfect table settings: easy and elegant ideas for hundreds of napkin folds and table arrangements / Denise Vivaldo.

Includes index.

ISBN 978-0-7788-0254-9

    1. Table setting and decoration. 2. Napkins. I. Title.

TX879.V58 2010   642'.7   C2010-903195-4

Index

Note: Bold type is used to indicate recipe titles and the locations of napkin-folding instructions.